· CRIME WATCHING ·

CRIME WATCHING

Investigating Real Crime TV

Deborah Jermyn

I.B. TAURIS

LONDON · NEW YORK

Published in 2007 by I.B.Tauris & Co Ltd
6 Salem Road, London W2 4BU
175 Fifth Avenue, New York NY 10010
www.ibtauris.com

In the United States of America and Canada
distributed by Palgrave Macmillan a division of St Martin's Press
175 Fifth Avenue, New York NY 10010

Hardback   ISBN: 978 1 84511 238 7
Paperback ISBN: 978 1 84511 239 4

A full CIP record for this book is available from the British Library
A full CIP record is available from the Library of Congress

Library of Congress Catalog Card Number: available

Typeset in Palatino by JCS Publishing Services
Printed and bound in Great Britain by TJ International, Padstow,
Cornwall

Contents

· For Julia Jermyn ·
for everything

Acknowledgements

While carrying out the research for this book I have been fortunate enough to work with wonderful colleagues at the Southampton Institute and Roehampton University. Thanks in particular to Cathy Fowler, David Lusted, Karen Randell and Sean Redmond for their friendship and intellectual camaraderie; Anita Biressi and Heather Nunn for generously sharing their TV archive; Susie Hyde and TVR for helping me build my own; Stacey Abbott for always being a top 'roomie'; and Su Holmes, for being the most insightful of readers, the most diligent of shoppers and the dearest of friends. I am grateful to Philippa Brewster at I.B.Tauris for supporting this project and for providing one of the highlights of (my) Glastonbury 2003 with her phone call commissioning this book. Thanks also to Roberta Pearson and Cindy Carter who provided invaluable commentary on this work in its early stages, as did Charlotte Brunsdon; I am especially indebted to Charlotte too for being an inspiring teacher and writer, and for the endless encouragement she has given me over the years. Former colleagues at New Scotland Yard continued to assist me after my return to academia, my particular thanks go to Stephanie Day and Nikki Redmond. I am also tremendously grateful to all the production personnel at the BBC and ITV who generously gave up their time to give me the interviews that have enormously enriched my research; thanks to Katie Thomson, Belinda Phillips, Jo Scarratt and Tim Miller. Finally, thanks also to my 'partners in crime' for always providing such interesting diversions away from the computer – to Fab, Kath, Steph, Tom, the two Abs, Law, Cath, Nova, Ryanne, Adam, Pam, Pat, Jules, Nick, Shân, Michael, Harad, Bella, Lisa, Portia and Steve especially – this summer I have realised more than ever how blessed I am to call you my friends.

Part of Chapter 3 was previously published in 'Photo Stories and Family Albums: Imaging Criminals and Victims on *Crimewatch UK*', in Paul Mason (ed.), *Criminal Visions: Media Representations of Crime and Justice*, Devon: Willan, 2003. Part of Chapter 4 was previously published in '"This is About Real People!"; Video Technologies, Actuality and Affect in the Television Crime Appeal', in Su Holmes and Deborah Jermyn (eds), *Understanding Reality Television*, London: Routledge, 2004, and part of the Conclusion was previously published in the Introduction to *Understanding Reality Television*.

DJ
August 2005

Introduction

Nicola Speller & Deborah Jermyn at the New Scotland Yard radio studio, London, 1995. (Published in *Metropolitan Journal*, 1995, pp. 32–3 © Metropolitan Police.)

· RETURNING TO A SCENE OF CRIME ·

The picture above features my former colleague, Nicola Speller, and myself in the radio studio of New Scotland Yard in 1995.

We were both working there as press officers with particular responsibility for media crime appeals. Specifically, my job entailed looking out for and helping to publicise crime stories in London, where a public appeal might prove particularly helpful to the investigation. As such, I was the central Metropolitan Police contact for *Crimewatch UK* (BBC, 1984–) (hereafter abbreviated to *Crimewatch*) and the ITV equivalent at that time, *Crime Monthly* (London Weekend Television – LWT, 1989–96). Nicola and I also used to do a twice-daily live radio appeal called 'Police Call', broadcast on London News Radio, hence our picture in the radio studio. It was taken to accompany a piece I had written for the Met's in-house *Metropolitan Journal* called 'An Appealing Solution' (Jermyn, 1995), an article in which I explained the value of crime appeals in an attempt to persuade police officers to contact us if they had a crime that would be appropriate for such publicity.

There's something else I should say about this photo.

It's a fake.

Of course, it's real in that it really is me and I really did that job and really worked in that studio. But it's also an elaborate con-struction, a fabrication, an image devised purely for publication. The details of this image were carefully selected and manipulated by the photographer; and I was complicit in the deception.

As you can see, Nicola and I are sitting in front of two monitors, placed on the shelf above us. In fact, our real desk was to the right of this. The monitors weren't ours and we never used them in our job – they were showing images from traffic cameras used by the radio station GLR for their live traffic reports. You'll note that Nicola's got her headphones on and is holding a script and pen, as if she's updating it and is just about to go on-air; needless to say, she wasn't. There's a video player on the shelf too and I'm holding a video-tape, poised for action, ready to view some manner of har-rowing police footage for use in the fight against crime. But the video player wasn't plugged in and we'd never watched videos in this space. We'd brought it downstairs from another office at the behest of the photographer to place meaningfully on the shelf.

There's also a clock on the desk dominating the frame in the middle, stressing the urgency of our job, the perpetual nature of our appeal work. Actually, it had been taken off the wall above so it could be seen in the picture. The way we have been asked to pose also has a significant effect; our bodies face towards the equip-ment and our heads are turned backwards, as if we've just been interrupted at our desk in the middle of something – but of course, we hadn't.

As I explain the background to this picture and detail the real context in which it was taken, an unavoidable irony leaps out: that though this is a genuine picture taken from the real nerve centre of London's police service, perhaps the most famous police headquarters in the world, it's not entirely 'real'. It seems ironic too, that the audience for this picture were the police themselves – the *Metropolitan Journal* was distributed to serving officers – so that it is the very people actually engaged in fighting crime that the photographer sought to convince of our efforts through this simulacrum. Somehow, for our photographer the image as it 'really' was wasn't real enough and had to be supplemented and enhanced. A few minor additions and props, a certain kind of body language, a foregrounding of time and the suggestion of being 'caught' in the midst of the job, together succeeded in bringing a greater sense of technological know-how, urgency and dynamism to the image than was there, in actuality, to begin with.

· CULTURAL CRITICISM AS DETECTION ·

I open this book with this picture for numerous reasons. Partly, it seems apt because it was taken during a year spent in a job that spurred my academic interest in crime and the media. But I also show it because, in a book that is often concerned with the nature of TV crime appeal reconstructions, it seems appropriate to open with a picture that is in effect a kind of reconstruction. Why was it that the photographer sought out those props – props that, in 'reality', didn't belong there? How did he think his picture might otherwise disappoint? He clearly had expectations about what a police radio studio should look like, and we didn't live up to it. Arguably these expectations and the narrative themes they suggest – that sense of urgency, technological capability and actu- ality – were as much drawn from his knowledge and experience of crime *fiction* as from his having visited real police offices. In this way, this photo is not just a reconstruction; it is also the scene of a 'crime'. As popular discourses about representation in real crime TV would have it, a kind of fraud has taken place in this 'blurring of boundaries'; indeed, this notion of 'blurring' is a theme that this book will return to throughout its investigation. Hence, this image demonstrates, contributes to and perpetuates the operation of a familiar cycle regarding media representations of crime. The photographer here – a mediator of crime stories and images – seems to draw on knowledge gained and merged from fictional and real life representations and experience of crime and crime-fighting in order to construct his work; an image likely to be largely read as authentic. What TV drama(s) had he seen, what newspaper testimonies had he read that led him to believe that a studio where police personnel deliver radio crime appeals should appear more industrious, more pressurised, than ours actually did?

In the process of making this picture from the position of being a Metropolitan Police photographer – a position that ostensibly carries a privileged degree of access to 'the real' – an image such as this (which, like any image, is indelibly constructed and manipulated) is presented, and enters into circulation, as being 'real'. Of course, human intervention into the manipulation of 'actuality' images within the practice of photography is as old as photography itself. Still, what this picture points to is the movement, manipulation and permeability of generic motifs across real life and fictional media representations of crime as a whole. This fluidity, around the way 'crime fiction' and 'real life' crime are constructed on contemporary TV, is one of the key interests in what follows in this book.

To elaborate, this book looks at the growth of real crime TV in Britain in recent years, arguing that the birth of *Crimewatch* in 1984 was a key transitional moment in the emergence, expansion and popularity of this kind of television programming, both in the UK and internationally. Because of this, *Crimewatch* takes a privileged and central position in this book.[1] It is conceptualised as a platform from which one can usefully begin to examine and understand the massive subsequent success of real crime TV that followed it and it is returned to throughout in order to illustrate and interrogate the pleasures, attractions and durability of real crime narratives in popular culture. As soon as *Crimewatch* was picked up by the BBC, from which time it quickly became a staple component of Britain's major public service broadcaster, the stage was set for this spectacular and highly visible genre to embed itself in UK television schedules. A look at the terrestrial TV listings for just one week in the UK, 12–18 April 2003, demonstrates just how ubiquitous crime programming is in our contemporary schedules. In addition to British and American crime dramas such as *Law and Order* (Channel 5 – 5), *The Bill* (ITV1), *CSI: Miami* (5), *CSI; Crime Scene Investigation* (5), *The Sopranos* (Channel 4 – C4) *Boomtown* (5), *NYPD Blue* (C4) and *Midsomer Murders* (ITV1), there were a wealth of various 'real crime' programmes to be seen. These included *Murder Detectives* (5); *The Hunt for Jill Dando's Killer* (C4); *The Real Blair Witch* (C4) (a documentary on the kidnap and death of a woman in Michigan), *Crime and Punishment* (5) (featuring real life US court cases), *To Catch a Thief* (BBC1) (featuring advice on how to burglar-proof one's home), *McIntyre – UK Undercover* (5) (investigating credit card fraud) and *Danielle Cable: Eyewitness* (ITV1) (a 'factual drama' recreating a 1996 road-rage murder). As this selection demonstrates, there are a number of more specific genres or programme types contained within the umbrella term of 'real crime TV'; for example, crime appeal programmes, which seek public help with unsolved crimes; reconstruction programmes, which re-enact solved crimes; and actuality footage programmes, which provide montages of police, CCTV, hidden-camera or public footage of crimes being undertaken. 'Real crime TV' is used here to cover this fairly broad spectrum of programmes which either show filmed extracts of crimes taking place or reconstruct real crimes. Police presenters or interviews with police are a common feature in all these programmes, functioning to enhance the programmes' sense of a privileged access to and close relationship with those who move at the frontline of real crime, thereby enhancing the programme's own sense of authenticity. In what follows, then, I look closely at the emergence of *Crimewatch*, the social and political context of the period in which it first appeared and the reasons for its continued success, while also examining the aesthetics, audience address and appeal of some of the proliferation of programmes coming in its wake, such as *America's Most Wanted*, *Cops*, *Crime Monthly*, *Britain's Most Wanted*, *America's Dumbest Criminals*, *Police Camera Action!*, *World's Wildest Police Videos*, *SWAG*, *Rat Trap*, and *Shops, Robbers and Videotape*.

I also open with this picture, since my analysis of it mirrors aspects of my broader methodology throughout this book. By returning to the 'scene of the crime', examining this photo and exposing the deception that it makes, by unearthing the clues contained within, I become a kind of detective. The title of this book describes the work that follows as an *'investigation'* of real crime TV. The approach I open with – making close textual analysis of an image which takes this (and any) text to be a form of evidence that is better understood through detailed semiological dissemination of its construction – is one I adopt throughout. Furthermore, one of the arguments I make here is that photos and photographic technology are one of the most fundamental and evocative components of crime appeal programming that are integral to the form (note how the photographer in my opening image insisted we be pictured next to the screens showing scenes drawn from CCTV traffic cameras, though these were completely immaterial to our job). My textual analysis is in this sense partly informed by John Hartley's concept of 'forensic analysis', where the text and its related intertexts become 'material evidence'. In *The Politics of Pictures* (1992), Hartley borrows from the approach of forensic science, which is to search for truth based on clues, to turn objects into subjects, to transform the facts of physics and chemistry into the language of discourse and argument. In forensic analysis, objects are 'caused to talk as mute witnesses ... coaxed into telling a story' (Hartley, 1992: 28). Such an approach is highly apposite to this work, first, in that I am approaching the programmes under discussion with the aim of reconstructing the 'bigger picture', the social and televisual context, of which they are fragments. Second, this approach engages with the language of forensics, which is itself taken up within some of the discourses featured in these programmes. Furthermore, Hartley's own context, the place where he puts the methodology of forensic analysis to work, is the *interrogation of pictures*. This is particularly potent here, then, in that, as indicated above, I will argue in my discussion of TV crime appeals that the circulation and dissemination of the photographs of victims and criminals is one of the genre's most characteristic and central motifs. As Susan Sontag's seminal study of photography commented, 'Photographs furnish evidence. Something we hear about but doubt, seems proven when we're shown a photograph of it' (1979: 5). I suggest that the use of photographic technologies is arguably the most visible signifier of realism in *Crimewatch* and other crime appeal and real crime shows, and my analysis of their use will be a central component of my discussion of the programme.

My analysis of the New Scotland Yard photo also points to the importance that institutional contextualisation can have for enriching our understanding of the text. The information and insight I can bring to bear as someone who collaborated on the making of the photo might supplement, enhance or even contradict that which I may bring to bear on it as an 'objective' cultural critic, opening up a degree of dialogue which might lead to a more informed mode of analysis. One of the most important interventions this project makes in comparison to other work undertaken to date on *Crimewatch* is that it is informed, at least to some extent, by production and industry perspectives. This is partly in terms of the knowledge gained in my period as a media crime appeals press officer at New Scotland Yard and partly, and more significantly, in the interviews I have been able to undertake with a number of different leading production personnel making crime appeal programmes on contemporary British television.[2] These interviews provide at least a partial sense of some of the institutional, televisual and other prerogatives shaping these programmes for those that actually make them. No other academic analysis of *Crimewatch* to date has enjoyed such an extensive degree of access to the commentaries of industry figures or attempted to contextualise its findings in the light of such material. The result is a more expansive and multi-perspectival account than is very often the case within Television Studies, where engagement with industry personnel is still, surprisingly, something of a rarity, a neglect which is something else this work seeks partly to address.

We might say, finally, that this photo is the first in a series of forms of 'intertextual evidence' that I draw on here. This is a phrase formulated by Urrichio and Pearson (1993: 4) which, with its attention to the notion of cultural artefact as '*evidence*', seems to share the same spirit of cultural criticism as an investigative process seen in Hartley's 'forensic analysis'. In privileging such material I seek to contextualise these programmes by approaching them not just through isolated scrutiny of the text itself, but alongside analysis of a number of cultural artefacts that have engaged in some shape or form with it. As Uricchio and Pearson note in *Reframing Culture,* 'Textual analysis tells us nothing about reception' (1993: 4). Thus their work demonstrates how in order best to understand the 'interface' between media and culture it is necessary to draw on a much broader series of evidence than the primary text itself. Hence I take my intertextual evidence to include popular reviews, industry research papers, newspaper articles, interviews, 'spin-off' books and so on. Such evidence is never transparent; it can not in itself crystallise a historical moment or provide some kind of direct access to a definitive grasp of a socio-political context. Rather, such evidence must be approached with a consciousness of the fact that it is shaped by its own institutional and media contexts and an awareness of the influence of one's own research objectives. As Hartley's forensic analysis contends, 'the politics of pictures' commences 'with their *status*; what their status is determines how their textual and social politics will be understood and conducted, but their status *is not self-evident*. On the contrary, it is a product of *the way they are looked at*' (1992: 30, my italics).

It is the attention I give to close textual analysis of the television text here that is perhaps one of the most distinctive elements of this book. Detail about the text can sometimes seem strangely lacking in television analysis, arguably because in many ways – even with the rise in video technology over the last two decades, and more recently the proliferation of TV series on DVD – the TV text is still more ephemeral than, for example, the cinematic text. Furthermore, of course, there is a cultural hierarchy within television, where only a certain kind of 'quality' television, quite distinct from much of the programming under discussion here, predominantly warrants wide preservation and distribution on DVD. For the bulk of the history of Television Studies there seems to have been an understandable reluctance, then, for analysts to give detailed textual analysis of a specific instance of a given programme in much of Television Studies, given that any particular example may prove transient and not be readily available to others again. In the late 1980s Charlotte Brunsdon (1989) partly attributed the tendency for the neglect of the text by Television

Studies to its preoccupation around this time with *the audience* as its primary focus. Some recent work such as Karen Lury's *Interpreting Television* (2005) suggests a sea change where this neglect of close textual analysis is being increasingly addressed The approach I adopt here indicates the validity and legitimacy of turning detailed attention to the mechanisms of the text itself, while demonstrating the ways in which a critical understanding of the television text and its audience(s) can be constructed from a range of 'evidence'. This approach, then, incorporates a range of institutional, textual and theoretical perspectives, to indicate the diverse ways in which we can seek to understand and conceptualise the television text.

At this juncture it would be instructive to establish briefly some of the key facets of *Crimewatch*'s history and format. The programme was introduced by the BBC in 1984 and was a unique venture at this time in that it was the first British crime appeal programme to be transmitted live and to feature both civilian and police presenters. Its crime appeal function was/is pursued in a variety of different sub-formats; filmed reconstructions of unsolved crimes; studio appeals where briefer synopses of crimes are given by the civilian presenters; 'named faces' where wanted criminals are identified and assistance on their whereabouts requested; and video, CCTV and still photos of unidentified criminals where help with identification is sought (these latter two sub-formats generally introduced by police presenters). Filmed reconstructions are always supported by interviews with family or friends of the victims and with the investigating officer, as indeed are studio appeals in many instances. The appeals are also supplemented by updates (formerly called 'Your Call Counts'), which give developments on previously featured crimes. My analysis argues that *Crimewatch* must be recognised as a pivotal text in recent British television history and in the development of real crime TV for a number of reasons. First, for its status as a distinctive form of televisual text that has proved enduringly popular with audiences; second, as a potent, influential and highly visible determinant in its viewers' relationship with crime and in the massive growth of crime programming in television schedules over the last two decades; and finally as a text that crystallises a whole array of issues and preoccupations that lie at the core of major social and televisual shifts occurring in Britain over this period – interests subsequently taken up by the wider real crime TV movement it precipitated.

Now Britain's most successful and longest-running television crime appeal programme, *Crimewatch* holds a familiar, conspicuous and significant place in contemporary British culture. Its resonance is evident in the way in which it has been widely parodied or mimicked in other TV texts, from the gritty police drama *Prime Suspect* (ITV, 1991) to cult comedy *Phoenix Nights* (C4, 2002) to the 'Conwatch' adverts for UKTV Gold's summer comedy season (2005). There are few viewers with even a passing familiarity with the show who couldn't complete presenter Nick Ross's famous sign-off 'catch-phrase', 'Don't have nightmares. Do sleep well'. While it may now be over two decades old, *Crimewatch*'s impact remains highly visible, both in the way in which it has popularised commonly held perceptions about crime in Britain and in the manner in which our current televisual landscapes, in the UK and internationally, have evolved to become increasingly dominated by 'reality TV' formats.

The aesthetics, narrative terrain and popularity of *Crimewatch* mark it as a key forerunner to the current reality TV movement, even though in the UK's contemporary televisual marketplace it would no longer be among the most obvious contenders to bear the mantle of 'reality TV'. Nevertheless, Richard Kilborn's early work on 'Recent Developments in "Reality' Television"' (1994) included it in his discussion. Similarly, Hugh Dauncey's 1996 discussion of 'French Reality Television' referred to *Témoin No. 1* – the French equivalent of *Crimewatch UK* – as 'the doyen of French reality shows' (1996: 91). Elsewhere, current work from the US (Cavender, 2004) unequivocally refers to the US equivalent, *America's Most Wanted*, as 'reality TV'. Indeed, Kilborn's discussion rather failed to knowledge just how influential a precursor *Crimewatch* (and indeed by extension *Aketenzeichen XY ... Ungelost*, the German programme on which *Crimewatch* was based) was to the movement he examines. He suggests that 'the original stimulus for RP [Reality Programming] came from the United States ... NBC were the first company to get in on the reality act with their *Unsolved Mysteries* (1987)', while other networks soon followed suit with police/emergency services based reality shows such as *America's Most Wanted* on Fox (Kilborn, 1994: 426). This neglects the fact that *Crimewatch* first appeared some three years earlier, in 1984, and that, rather than *Unsolved Mysteries*, it was arguably *Crimewatch* that provided the principal inspiration for *America's Most Wanted* (as indeed it did for *Témoin No. 1*). As a leading light in the BBC's stable of established and popular series, *Crimewatch* also has much to tell us about the place of public service broadcasting and its relationship with commercial television since the programme's inception. Equally, analysis of *Crimewatch* and real crime TV leads one to engage with a series of issues that suggest a great deal about the enduring and persistent nature of our fascination with crime stories and criminality, as well as more contemporaneous concerns about the future of television and its role as a cultural marker of our times.

· FOCUSING THE ENQUIRY – CRIME WATCHING ·

This book opens in Chapter 1 by contextualising *Crimewatch* within some of the key televisual and political frameworks at work in Britain and British television in the mid-1980s, all of which start to account for why *this* programme came to our screens at *this* time.[3] Following an examination of *Police 5* as a precursor to *Crimewatch*, I examine the socio-political context in which *Crimewatch* emerged. These were the years of Margaret Thatcher's Conservative government, an era where the police were growing increasingly PR conscious and a period that was overtly concerned with law and order politics (part of a broader rhetoric fearing a decline in moral standards that owes much to debates that were prominent too in the late 1950s and 1960s). Exploring the ways in which the programme situates and addresses its audience as citizens, and comparing this too with *America's Most Wanted*, I examine how it makes a distinctive appeal to 'community' and link this in part to the political zeitgeist of the era and in part to the BBC's public service remit. Analysis here demonstrates how the programme avoids contextualising crime and instead nurtures both an intimate relationship with the police and a mode of address that pivots on a nostalgic and reaffirming appeal to community, an ideal that is perceived as under threat in this era. These characteristics are fundamental components in *Crimewatch*'s identity and mark it as largely conservative in its operation, generally endorsing police work (something symptomatic of real crime TV as a whole) while deflecting attention away from serious social debate through a focus on its own tangible results.

In Chapter 2, I contextualise crime appeal programming further by exploring its place in the emotive and heavily contentious 'fear of crime' debates that were circulating around British television in the mid-1980s to early 1990s, and reflect on the meanings of these anxieties about crime and television. This is done in part through a comparative analysis of *Crimewatch* with other leading crime appeal programmes, LWT's *Crime Monthly* and ITV's *Britain's Most Wanted* (ITV, 1998–2000), which are also examined in têrms of the wider issues raised by channel identity and commercial versus public service broadcasting. While *Crimewatch* may have weathered the storm of this controversial period, outliving its rivals, I examine how, nevertheless, it is often party to constructing a thrilling, sensationalist viewing experience that is pronounced across the contemporary crime appeal format.

In Chapters 3 and 4 I examine how the emergence and success of *Crimewatch* and the wider real crime movement that followed was enabled by, and very much continues to pivot on, the attractions and capabilities of certain photographic technologies. Chapter 3 looks initially at the importance of *still* photography to the crime appeal format, remaining a cornerstone of *Crimewatch* and its compatriots, despite the growth of new technologies. This leads also to discussion of temporality in the programme and specifically the conjunction of studio liveness with the 'that has been'-ness of photography (Barthes, 1993: 77). While the expansion of real crime TV was greeted by critics as indicative of a 'new' phenomenon, I demonstrate here that this fascination with the spectacle of criminal stories, with rendering criminals visible, has a long history in popular culture that real crime TV merely attenuates.[3] I contextualise the programme's use of images of criminals by situating it within the historical association that has long existed between photography and criminal apprehension, a relationship particularly borne out by the relatively contemporaneous development in the mid-nineteenth century of photography and increasingly more sophisticated police detection practices. Images of *victims* in the programme fulfil a set of curiosities and cultural uses rather different to the purpose of images of the criminal. Here, I examine how the programme utilises the traditions of the 'family album', how photographs (and indeed video) of victims are often used to underline victims' familial ties, constructing them through these associations as legitimate victims and emphasising the significance of their loss *because* of these ties. Through its unquestioning endorsement of the institution of the family, we see again how the crime appeal format adheres to and promotes conventional and conservative ideologies surrounding gender roles, citizenry and law and order.

In Chapter 4, I look at how the rapid growth of CCTV and video as new technologies in the 1980s could be said to have both contributed to and reflected some of the apparent preoccupations of the era, providing novel, affordable 'actuality' footage for emergent real crime TV formats. As we see in Chapter 1, the introduction of *Crimewatch* and the growth of real crime programming was bound up in discourses and anxieties that were particularly prevalent at that time, regarding the perceived breakdown of community, growing crime and shifts in the nature of policing. Another feature of these debates – and another crucial factor in the emergence of *Crimewatch* and the growth of real crime TV – was the rise of CCTV, security cameras and video technology at this time. Hence, I examine debates regarding whether real crime TV has actually contributed to the expansion and normalisation of a surveillance culture, since as Biressi and Nunn note, the availability of CCTV footage 'turns every subject into a potential film subject, with or without their consent' (2005: 7). Real crime programming stands accused of helping to establish the 'everydayness' of CCTV and (arguably misleadingly) its reputation as a preventative measure in the fight against crime by embedding it in popular television. Alongside the international growth of so-called 'A and E' (Accident and Emergency) programming (Kilborn, 2003: 10), such as Fox's *Cops*, BBC1's *999* and CBS's *Rescue 911*, soon came the 'reality clipshow format' (Annette Hill, 2005: 8). These programmes are largely made up of unscripted actuality footage obtained by programme makers from police and witnesses to dangerous, amusing and otherwise spectacular incidents. Real crime clipshows have been largely understood as ideologically conservative, legitimising surveillance technologies and complicit in serving the interests of the police by showing them as infinitely heroic. While acknowledging the persuasiveness of this reading, I resituate the implications of the growth in clipshow programmes such as *Police Camera Action!* and *World's Wildest Police Videos*, by suggesting that we might understand these programmes to be less ideologically conservative in their function than their crime appeal predecessors, since the excess and spectacle of criminality is arguably foregrounded and relished with a far less overtly moral purpose/project.

In Chapter 5, I present an audience case study of real crime TV, in particular reflecting on the relationship between the crime appeal format and gender, by examining how the female viewer of *Crimewatch* has been constructed. This arena is particularly rich in material, and particularly significant for extending our understanding of the relationship between audiences and real crime TV, given the way that women have consistently featured as the real casualties of fear of crime. For example, the second British National Crime Survey in 1984, the year *Crimewatch* first came to our screens, found that 48% of women, compared to 13% of men, described themselves as feeling 'unsafe' (Gunter, 1987: 3). My analysis here critiques *Crimewatch* for promoting a misleading picture of the kinds of crime women are most likely to experience – stranger sex attacks – in reconstructions that are sometimes constructed in sensationalistic ways. Work by Schlesinger et al. (1992) and C. Kay Weaver (1998) has reached similar conclusions, suggesting that *Crimewatch* is part of a general discourse in the popular media about crime, which exhorts women to adopt certain (restricting) kinds of behaviour and encourages them to 'keep off the streets'. Nevertheless, I open this chapter by asking what are the *pleasures* of true crime, particularly for women, since this is an aspect of the female audience's engagement with real crime TV that critics have been reticent, if not resistant, to acknowledge and understand. I reflect on why women have been found to be the majority audience for numerous real crime TV shows, including not just *Crimewatch* but *America's Most Wanted* and *Unsolved*

Mysteries (Fishman, 1998). I then go on to examine how, mirroring the construction of fear of crime, the popular representation of the female *Crimewatch* viewer has situated her as 'vulnerable', even hysterical in her engagement with the programme. However, while acknowledging the real potency of the programme for women's fear of crime, I argue that women may also be using *Crimewatch* and other real crime TV as a strategy for *managing* their fear of crime; a reconfiguration of their engagement with the genre that endows them with agency rather than vulnerability.

In the final chapter of the book, I examine how one of the most recurrent critiques of real crime TV has been the accusation that it 'blurs boundaries', be that through mixing 'entertainment' formats with serious 'information'; through obscuring distinctions between police and civilian identities; or through the conflation of 'fact' and 'fiction'. I reflect on the reasons why this generic hybridity – whether in the form of drama-documentary, reconstructions, or documentary-drama – has such a long and controversial history in British television. I suggest that these fears perpetuate the tradition of the mass-society thesis with its suggestion that audiences are unable to cope in any discerning way with hybrid or internally complex forms (see Brooker and Jermyn, 2002: 5–6). The paternalistic and conservative impulses behind this critique of this kind of television become all the more telling in light of the fact that the audiences for numerous real crime TV programmes have been found to be predominantly female and/or working class (Fishman, 1998; Thomson, 2002). I argue that the concept of 'blurred boundaries' has less and less currency in the contemporary televisual climate, that we need to question the motives for our continuing critical and cultural discomfort around the loss of these 'distinctions'. It is now, then, that a concerted new appraisal of the 'boundaries' thought to be observed within and adopted by television as an organising principle warrants our attention. By moving beyond our preoccupation with 'blurring boundaries' we might more fruitfully come to understand television as a medium where these boundaries can not remain rigid and are instead consistently under construction and negotiation; and recognise that this is a process that is nowhere more evident than in real crime TV.

Surprisingly perhaps, relatively little work has sought to consider how 'real life' and 'fictional' representations of crime operate in conjunction with one another. By examining the nature of 'reconstructions' as a hybrid form that draws on both modes, this book underlines the importance of this relationship. Discussing the representation of women and violence in *No Angels; Women Who Commit Violence*, Alice Myers and Sarah Wight recognise the significance of this interaction when they note in their introduction:

> There is an intimate dialogue between reality and how it is presented. Fiction borrows from real life, and 'facts' can easily be compromised in the very process of reporting them ... Ultimately, the cultural meaning of stories of women's violence lies somewhere between reality and representation. (1996: xii)

It is in part this hazy territory, the place between reality and representation, that I investigate in what follows. By looking closely at the operation of reconstructions in crime appeals – arguably a form that more than any other lies in that space 'somewhere between reality and representation' – this book contributes further to this field of study. Interestingly, Ngaire Naffine has argued that the work of crime fiction and criminology are far closer than one might initially think. Both are about 'meaning-making' and, of course, in neither instance is meaning natural or given. Criminologists, much like the creators of crime fiction, are engaged in the process of constructing and constituting a body of knowledge, a series of meanings; as such they are part of the chain of ideology, not merely 'objectively' reporting crime but passing on ingrained ideological assumptions. Therefore, Naffine argues for the need to understand criminology as a 'process of invention' that must look to other disciplines for a greater awareness of its own creativity:

> If the making of meaning is already a creative process, then there is no hard division between the creative nature of writing about crime fact and the creativity involved in crime fiction ... once we view the study of crime as a process of invention rather than the simple discovery of what is already in place, then the division between fact and fiction begins to break down ... disciplinary boundaries do not hold in a firm or abiding manner. (1997: 122–3)

In a similar vein, then, to Naffine's call for a greater awareness of the shared processes of meaning-making across criminology and crime fiction, this book in part reflects on how in real crime TV the perceived discreteness of fictional and real life discourses are shown to be increasingly indistinguishable. Instead, these discourses operate broadly in remarkably similar ways, recurrently adopting the same kinds of language, images and narrative strategies.

In brief then, in what follows I make the single most detailed analysis of *Crimewatch* undertaken to date, while recognising and exploring its enormous influence on the international real crime TV movement; contextualising the growth of real crime TV within the historical and socio-political frameworks of Britain in the 1980s; critically examining the media's vocal and emotive concerns about both television and fear of crime and television's alleged 'blurring' of narrative boundaries and distinctions between 'fact' and 'fiction'; undertaking detailed analysis of the pivotal role of surveillance, CCTV and photographic technologies to the genre and the concomitant rise of a 'surveillance culture'; interrogating the crime appeal's conservative and repressive representation of female victims and extending work on the ideological ramifications of this through more expansive analysis of the construction of its 'hysterical' female viewer; reconfiguring and extending feminist analysis by looking too at the notion of the female audience's *pleasure* and investment in true crime narratives; and exploring the ways that critical approaches to real crime TV might now usefully move forward. What all this points to and reveals is a genre rich in contradictory and conflictual impulses, calling on cultural convention, tradition and historical association while simultaneously being embedded in the preoccupations and cultural transitions of its times; endorsing conventional and conservative ideological structures while affording subversive pleasure in spectacles of actuality and criminality; all of which goes some way towards accounting for the remarkable rise of real crime TV in recent years and its transformation of our television schedules.

· NOTES ·

1 The core sample of *Crimewatch* is drawn from January–June 2000, supplemented by reference to numerous editions from 2000–5, while a variety of episodes of the diverse real crime programmes outlined here are also drawn on.

2 On 2 April 2001 I interviewed Jo Scarratt, producer, and Tim Miller, series producer, of *Britain's Most Wanted* – both formerly producers of *Crime Monthly* – at the LWT offices in London. On 22 January 2002 I interviewed Katie Thomson, series producer of *Crimewatch UK* and on 19 February 2002 I interviewed Belinda Phillips, assistant producer of *Crimewatch UK*, both at BBC TV offices, Wood Lane, London.

3 Clearly, precedents for real crime TV can be traced back long before the mid-1980s; as Anita Biressi notes, 'Real life crime has been a source of narrative entertainment in both literature and popular entertainment since at least the early modern period' (2001: 45), evident in the popular murder pamphlets produced as early as the sixteenth century. Space prohibits me from engaging with any of these forms in any detail here, but Biressi provides a useful historical overview.

1 The Birth of *Crimewatch UK*
CONTEXTUALISING THE RISE OF REAL CRIME TV

The significance *Crimewatch* would come to hold as a major precursor to the real crime TV movement was never imagined back in 1984, when the programme was initially scheduled to run for just three episodes. The popularity of the show ensured this run was quickly extended and by 1987 its success was such that the programme's then presenters, Nick Ross and Sue Cook, published a book, *Crimewatch UK*, celebrating the series. The inside cover blurb pondered, '*Crimewatch UK* is Britain's top rated *factual TV series* with an audience of millions ... why has this *serious information programme* become more popular than most *entertainment* shows?' (Ross and Cook, 1987: inside cover, my italics).

These thoughts revealed much about how the programme viewed itself at that time. The word entertainment is assiduously avoided in relation to its own project. Instead this is a 'factual' programme, it is serious about providing 'information', wholeheartedly situating itself within the more sombre aspect of the BBC's public service broadcasting remit that requires it to 'inform, educate and entertain'. An implicit dichotomy is evident in their pitch: 'factual' programming, which is 'serious' in nature, is fundamentally distinguished from other kinds of television and specifically the popularity of 'entertainment shows'. Yet, as this blurb is also at pains to emphasise, it *is* also massively popular (achieving up to 13 million viewers). Audience-ratings researchers in the 1990s even coined the term '*the Crimewatch effect*' to account for the fact that once a month the BBC's *9 O'Clock News* crept into the TV top 30; the extra numbers were explained by the anticipation of audiences tuning in early for the edition of *Crime-watch* that followed (Fiddick, 1992: 31). Would such numbers be tuning in regularly if 'information' alone was on offer? And as a national programme, how 'informative' can *Crimewatch* really claim to be, given that by its very nature it deals with regional crimes and appeals? Its continued success after more than two decades surely indicates that in *Crimewatch,* entertainment and information are intricately inter-related. More perceptive than the blurb above, in this respect, were the comments of John Stalker, the former deputy chief constable of Greater Manchester, two years after the publication of the *Crimewatch* book: 'neither viewers nor programme-makers have been able to define the point at which public service ends and entertainment begins ...' (cited in Woffinden, 1989: 10).

The promotional blurb indicates an early recognition of the way that 'fact' and 'fiction' collide in this format, most notably via reconstructions, and one cannot separate the fiction/entertainment function from the fact/information function of *Crimewatch* quite as readily as the writers above assumed. In interview, series producer Katie Thomson was frank about this juggling act and the challenges and paradoxes it produces for the programme makers. In the first instance, the programme is required to attract viewers in order to make its place in the television schedule and controversial intervention into police work justifiable. Equally, given that it is dealing with 'real crime' and the associated ethical and moral issues, it must not fall into over-dramatisation as a means of achieving this end. But as Thomson acknowledged, if it isn't 'entertaining' enough, people won't watch. In her words, 'We need people to watch to be witnesses. It's a constant concern. You have to make it interesting enough for people to watch without ever becoming gratuitous. And it's hard to get that balance right sometimes' (Thomson, 2002).

Notions surrounding pleasure, genre boundaries, audience address and the identities of public service versus commercial television are all themes crucial to a discussion of *Crimewatch* and all are implicitly raised by the series book's blurb above. Before going on to pursue these themes in the first two chapters here, I lay the foundations for analysis of *Crimewatch* by contextualising its arrival on British TV screens: first, alongside other precedents and parallels on television at this time and second, within the socio-political context and popularisation of Thatcherite discourses in the mid-1980s. Emerging in an era when a preoccupation with law and order and concerns regarding community and individual (versus social) responsibility were high on the cultural agenda, I suggest that this zeitgeist very much set the scene for the arrival of *Crimewatch* and the growth of real crime TV in the UK. I argue that these themes are made visible in the particular discourses that characterise *Crimewatch*'s mode of address, an address that I refer to as marked by the re-inscription of community, and the intimate partnership with police that it fosters.

· 1984 – THE BIRTH OF *CRIMEWATCH* ·

At this point, then, we must reflect on the particularities of the era in which *Crimewatch* appeared, since this was arguably a transitional moment in the subsequent growth of both the TV crime appeal and the broader genre of real crime programming that has arisen since then. Clearly, there are other wider, historical origins or influences that also warrant recognition alongside the specificities of the 1980s. For example, Annette Hill has examined how the broader reality TV movement draws 'on the staple ingredients of tabloid journalism, such as the interplay between ordinary people and celebrities, or information and entertainment' and points to *America's Most Wanted* (which took its inspiration largely from *Crimewatch*) as a good example of this (2005: 15). Given that one of the cornerstones of 'tabloidism' is the notion of 'ordinary people' caught up in 'extraordinary' events, *Crimewatch*'s diet of sensational, tragic and personal stories, of lives changed forever by crime, does indeed seem to draw heavily on some of the values of tabloid journalism. Nevertheless, Biressi has similarly noted that the growth of true crime literature in the same period can in part be attributed to, or seen as an extension of, the popularisation of more particular discourses that had come to dominate the British political landscape since the late 1970s. She argues,

> Analysis of contemporary true crime narratives offers insights into the kinds of power relations produced by the discourses of law and order, citizenship and individual responsibility and how these are articulated in popular literature. The recent forms of these relations of power, embodied in Thatcherite discourses of individual responsibility and law and order rose to prominence at the same time as true crime found significant commercial success. This conjunction invites the question of how true crime (and forms adjacent to it) articulates the nature of Thatcherism and its ideological legacy. (Biressi, 2001: 11)

Like any text, then, the emergence of *Crimewatch* in 1984 needs to be situated in the context of a range of social, historical and institutional factors pertinent to understanding why it evolved when it did. This is not to say that Thatcherism, or real crime TV, were entirely 'new'. In the words of Hall and Jacques, 'Political formations do not arise out of thin air. Thatcherism has deep roots in the political traditions of the right'; as, for example, the right-wing offensive against the so-called 'age of permissiveness' testified (1983: 10).

· KEEPING 'EM PEELED – *POLICE 5* ·

The legacy of this earlier period from the late 1950s and 1960s, then, may in part account for the advent of *Crimewatch*'s key British televisual precedent; *Police 5,* a nationally syndicated crime appeal slot that ran on LWT for 30 years from 1962 to 1992. However, while both programmes collaborate(d) with police in order to issue public crime appeals for information on unsolved crimes, they were in many ways rather different. *Crimewatch* had/has a monthly/three-weekly 50–60 minute slot broadcast live on BBC1 featuring a number of civilian and police presenters. It includes a range of forms of appeal, including filmed reconstructions, interviews, stills and CCTV/video footage and updates (formerly introduced with a 'Your Call Counts' logo) which report on the generally positive progress of previous cases, and is proceeded later the same evening by a live follow-up report, *Crimewatch UK Update. Police 5,* by comparison was a brief regional ITV programme pre-recorded and broadcast weekly (in just a five-minute slot). Shaw Taylor, who became known for his catch-phrase 'Keep 'em peeled!', produced, directed and presented the programme in the London region. A joint LWT and New Scotland Yard production, much of the programme took place in a very simple studio/office space where Taylor, framed in mid-shot, would deliver appeals to camera. He discussed clues and descriptions of suspects, introduced filmed footage of the locations and would sometimes be seen interviewing officers and revisiting the scene of the crime, though not actually 'reconstructing' the event. In Schlesinger and Tumber's words, it was 'more like a short news bulletin that a fully fledged programme' (1993: 19).

Given the brevity of the programme there was little time for introductions or elaborate denouement. For example, in the episode transmitted (hereafter abbreviated to tx) 3 October 1975, after a fleeting credit sequence, which features the *Police 5* logo superimposed over the image of a speeding police car driving along the urban streets at night, we cut straight to Shaw Taylor on the simple set, standing in front of a map which he points to as he establishes his first appeal. He tells us in brisk style that, 'This week, detectives in Kensington and Hackney are hoping that you'll be able to help with their investigation into two armed robberies ...'. This is followed by a series of exterior shots of buildings in the Notting Hill Gate area where, Shaw informs us in voiceover, employees were robbed of their office's salaries. Then there are a series of shots of a car driving the getaway route to illustrate the direction taken. At this point there is not even a voiceover; just the ambient noise of the car and other traffic. We then cut to a panning shot of the entrance to Holland Park, where we are told the car was dumped, followed by some pictures of the car. The overall style of this 'reconstruction', were we to call it that, is simple and arguably somewhat bland and dull (indeed the entire programme features only one voice – Taylor's). It consists of a series of stills and unimaginative shots that communicate the desired information, but do nothing to dramatise events or involve the viewer. Quite unlike *Crimewatch*, as we shall see, there are no 'characters' here, no personal stories, no cliffhangers or climaxes.

By the 1980s, *Police 5* had been enlivened somewhat. The episode tx 27 April 1986 demonstrates the programme had clearly developed and changed over the preceding decade. With an extended running time of 15 minutes, the programme was taking a little more time for embellishment. By this point, *Crimewatch* had been running for two years so it is difficult to tell to what extent these changes may be attributable to the appearance of its rival. We start with a more 'personal' touch from Taylor congratulating the audience for their input, a tone which, as we shall see, is certainly characteristic of *Crimewatch*. Opening this time with updates on three previously featured crimes he notes, 'In all three cases police have asked me to pass on thanks to *Police 5* viewers for their help in the investigations'. Two murder cases feature in this episode and in both instances we visit the scene of the crime with Taylor. In the first appeal, we learn that victim Harry Redhead was murdered on his way to a gig at the Town and Country Club. Taylor interviews the investigating officer on the street, who describes the victim's route that evening as we see abstract images of a man – his back, his legs – following the directions Harry took. As the officer describes the attack itself, we cut to a two-shot of the policeman and Taylor talking outside the pub where the victim's evening had begun, and end with a close-up of a passport photo of Harry as Taylor tells us, 'Harry Redhead died of his injuries'. Again, this is not quite a 'reconstruction' in the *Crimewatch* sense, merely revisiting the scene of crime and surrounding locale rather than recreating an entire series of events with actors, but the programme is at least not so relentlessly studio-bound as it had been.

The second murder appeal goes further to try and construct the victim as a 'character', a sympathetic figure with whom we might feel empathy, although, unlike *Crimewatch*, there are still no interviews with friends or family to aid this. We are told by Taylor in voiceover that 77-year-old Eileen Emms was murdered in her basement flat, after her killer wrenched off the cat flap at her home and broke in. This is accompanied by a shot of her house, with a shaky, handheld camera pushing through the bushes outside her window, as if mimicking the point of view of the intruder arriving there. Taylor tells us 'Frail, tiny 77-year-old Eileen Emms was a cat lover' and we cut to a picture of her standing outside her home in the drive with her cat near her feet. Staying focused on the picture, Taylor tells us she had lived at the house for 50 years, and that she'd been seen that day talking to a man on the drive. As we zoom into a close-up of the cat near her feet he comments, 'As you can see from this snapshot, she lived for her cats. It's ironic that they made her death possible.' This observation seems at best unintentionally facetious, at worst in poor taste, but appears to be a deliberate effort to add some drama to the proceedings, a twist to the tale.

We then cut to the interior of the victim's home and Taylor stands by the head of her bed as he describes how her home-help had arrived that morning and initially thought Eileen was sleeping in: 'It was only when she came back a little while later that she realised that Eileen Emms was dead. She'd been strangled.' There is something strangely sinister about him describing this as he stands with his hands on her headboard, a sentry guarding the very scene of the murder, where the killer himself must have stood. As Taylor wanders round Eileen's flat describing what is known about the events of that evening, he even pauses in the living room to peep under a covered plate, where a piece of bread lies, 'The remains of her supper', he comments dryly. Clearly all this is meant to enhance the drama, to add authenticity and a sense of how this was a real person's life cut down in the midst of an ordinary evening. It gives the eerie sensation of the victim having been there just a moment ago. But there is also something uncomfortably voyeuristic about it, since this wandering round her home is in many ways superfluous to solving the crime. There is no *need* to film the crime scene in this leisurely fashion, since there were no witnesses present at it. In short, the signs of a greater effort to personalise and dramatise these crimes is present. But the tenor of the show remains rather pedestrian and visually static, in a way that *Crimewatch* very much sought to evade.

Though it became something of an institution, *Police 5* was never a flagship show, and had nothing like the investment and production values of *Crimewatch*. Indeed, while it undoubtedly did much to heighten public awareness of crime and police work, while working as a Met Police Press Officer I was once told anecdotally that in London it was never directly responsible for the solving of a single specific featured crime.[1] Similar stories circulate about *Crimestoppers* (ITV 1988–95), another TV crime appeal format from the period, broadcast on regional daytime TV and featuring brief reconstructions in addition to crime prevention advice. However, while these programmes may not have been able to boast clear-up rates for specific crimes, what they *did* both achieve was a heightened awareness of the police's availability to the public and the pervasive nature of police work more generally; crucially, *Crimestoppers* publicised the national freephone number for the Crimestoppers initiative.

A registered charity in the UK, and a scheme which exists worldwide, Crimestoppers offers callers the opportunity to phone police anonymously any time, regarding any crime, with the possibility of receiving a reward for their information. It was launched in the UK in 1988, following the success of a scheme initiated in Albuquerque, New Mexico in 1976. A young man had been murdered at a filling station and though police suspected that locals were responsible and that people knew their identities, information had not been forthcoming. They set up an anonymous 'hotline' sponsored by local businesses and within 72 hours arrests were made. On their website Crimestoppers describe their 'vision':

> [To] become the most effective crime-solving tool in the country and to be perceived as such by communities and stakeholders. We will continue to reassure the public by increasing detections, therefore reducing crime and disorder and the fear of crime. We will engage the public in our activities, promoting an active citizenship. (www.crimstoppers_uk.org, accessed 13 August 2005)

As I go on to detail below, the language used here is very much bound up in the law and order discourses that were gaining momentum in the mid-1980s. It stresses the need to protect the interests of 'communities and stakeholders', demonstrates an awareness of the debilitating effects of 'fear of crime' as well as actual crime and sees crime fighting as an intrinsic element of good 'citizenship'. In this sense, the adoption of the scheme in the UK at this time arguably further evidences the social shift towards 'individual responsibility' and self-policing in this period.

Rather than being predominantly about appeals on specific crimes like *Police 5* and *Crimewatch*, a crucial element of the

Crimestoppers TV broadcasts was to promote general awareness of the scheme as a service where one might provide information on *any* criminal activity anonymously. Like these other crime appeal programmes, then, it fostered a new kind of relationship between the public and police that aimed to ease the process of 'informing' similarly. Certainly, New Scotland Yard detectives in the Crimestoppers office in London told me during the period I worked there that calls, on a wide range of crimes, would peak after a *Crimestoppers* TV appeal went out on the local London station, Carlton. In fact, along with *Crime Monthly* and later series like *Britain's Most Wanted* and *Rat Trap*, we might situate all these programmes within a growing culture of informing (or 'grassing' to use the British vernacular) gathering speed in this period. As Gareth Palmer notes,

> Since the early 1980s various agencies of the State have exhorted us to report crimes or any behaviour which look suspicious. A whole series of campaigns has been launched directed at licence fee avoidance, tax evasion, crime and, latterly, benefits fraud. The authorities have been anxious to spread the message that constant surveillance equates with good citizenship. (2003: 14)

Interestingly, in an illuminating instance of the significance of cultural specificity, the television crime appeal's endorsement of informing has been met by resistance elsewhere. Hugh Dauncey has in part attributed the controversy over and eventual demise of *Témoin No.* 1 ('Prime Witness') (1993–6), the French equivalent of *Crimewatch*, to 'concern over a possible revival in the French '"tradition" of informing, which dated to the period of collaboration' (1998: 198, see also Dauncey, 1996).

Of course, at least some of the information provided by callers to all these programmes leads to arrests. *Crimewatch* has always been at great pains to stress its 'clear-up' rate, since without this legitimising evidence of its value – without being seen to fulfil a tangible 'public service' in this way – it would lose its right to claim to be anything more lofty than entertainment. The programme's arrest and conviction rates feature on the website, are cited in interviews, spin-off programmes and books, though they are rarely specified in the programme itself. For instance, an episode featuring photos of 12 men wanted for rape introduced the item by noting '*Crimewatch* viewers have so far helped convict 57 rapists' (tx 13 April 2005). Interestingly, this acknowledgement of results is perhaps at its most pronounced in *America's Most Wanted*, where the start of every show features a rolling numerical update on arrests; 'To date your tips have led to the capture of 735 fugitives ...'. (tx 14 December 2002). Indeed, *Crimewatch*'s first producer, Peter Chafer, revealed the necessity of this when he said, 'Of course we need results, but for quite different reasons to policemen ... it would be insufferable if we showed chapter and verse and produced no results because critics could quite legitimately say that we were merely being exploitative' (cited in Schlesinger and Tumber, 1995: 262). The second *Crimewatch* book, *Crimewatch Solved – The Inside Story* (H. Miller, 2001), like the intermittent broadcast spin-offs *Crimewatch UK Solved* and *Crimewatch File* (BBC, 1988–) was purely dedicated to highlighting case-studies of some of the most celebrated successful convictions emanating from the programme, underlining that since 1984, '*Crimewatch* has been called in to help in over 2,000 cases and viewers' calls have resulted in more than 700 arrests' (Ross in H. Miller, 2001: 10). More recently, in July 2005 the *Crimewatch* website put this figure at 879 arrests (1 in 3) and 450 convictions (1 in 6) from a total of 2,923 cases featured.[2]

· THE QUEST FOR 'LAW AND ORDER' ·

Rather than *Police 5*, though, the most significant television precedent for *Crimewatch* is credited as having been a German show called *Aktenzeichen XY ... Ungelost,* roughly translated, 'Case XY ... Unsolved', which was spotted by a freelance TV researcher abroad who saw its potential for the UK market and brought a tape into the BBC (Ross and Cook, 1987: 9). This programme had begun in 1967 and enjoyed audiences of 'some 20 million in the Federal Republic, Austria and Switzerland' (Schlesinger and Tumber, 1995: 251). Its realisation and connotations there, however, were somewhat different to the UK incarnation in that it was actively drawn on in anti-terrorist appeals, thereby forging a link between the programme and political crime, something from which

Crimewatch chose from the onset to distance itself (Schlesinger and Tumber, 1995: 253). But clearly there was more than a drive for new programme initiatives behind the emergence of *Crimewatch*. As indicated above, it must also be situated within the social and political context of Britain in the mid-1980s and the Thatcher years.

The Conservative promise to prioritise and enforce 'law and order' was key to the political discourses of the time. Here, we must understand 'law and order' to encompass not just crime and justice policy and the work of particular agencies such as the police, courts and prisons, but also 'a much broader idea or attitude – even a sanction. It is a belief in and practice of *discipline* in attitudes, behaviour and choices in the home, the streets and the workplace' (Kettle, 1983: 219). This, then, was an era that was characterised by the demise of the 'nanny state' and a drive towards individual responsibility and independence and, by extension, self-policing – for example – this was also the period which popularised Neighbourhood Watch schemes (Palmer, 2003: 114). In Stuart Hall's words, the period's broader ideological project was to mark Thatcherism as 'a populist common sense'. He goes on, 'Thatcherite populism is a particularly rich mix. It combines the resonant themes of organic Toryism – nation, family, duty, authority, standards, traditionalism – with the aggressive theses of revived neo-liberalism – self-interest, competitive individualism, anti-statism' (Hall, 1983: 29).

Writing about *Aktenzeichen XY ... Ungelost*, Claus-Deiter Rath argues that crime appeal programmes operate by breaking down distinctions between police, state and public: 'The TV citizen becomes a member of the police, the restorer of "law-and-order", the eye of the law. The state and the police force merge into the audience' (1985: 200). One can see how much of this momentum coincides with Hall's account of the project of Thatcherite populism above. In a similar vein, Fairclough has argued in his detailed discourse analysis of an episode of *Crimewatch* from 1993 that the programme amounts to an 'intervention to shore up the crumbling public legitimacy of the state' (1995: 151). This description of the ideology behind the genre illuminates how the wider social context of Britain at this time might have facilitated the emergence of *Crimewatch*. The assimilation of police with public and programme makers was, of course, met with reservations in some quarters, partly because of concerns about the BBC's editorial independence, partly due to fears of the ramifications of the self-policing endorsed by the programme. *The Listener* asked 'Should the Corporation, and by implication its viewers, become a part of the police, an institution that is, after all, subject to criticism and debate?' (Woolley, 1984: 11).

Furthermore, the sense of growing social concern and consciousness of the possible prevalence and impact of crime in Britain was also evidenced in this period by the fact that the first British Crime Survey was carried out in 1981. In England and Wales 11,000 households and another 5,000 in Scotland were included, with a second survey being carried out only in England and Wales in 1984 (Gunter, 1987: 2) just as *Crimewatch* appeared on British screens for the first time. These surveys aimed to gain a fuller picture of crime than that offered by police statistics alone. It was hoped partly to unveil the extent of 'hidden' crimes that go unreported and thus do not figure in police statistics. Implicit in this was the recognition that such figures are always potentially flawed in that they 'may offer only a poor indication of the extent of crime, and reflect only a part of all the criminal activity that pervades society' (Gunter, 1987: 2). It is within the zeitgeist described here, then, that the birth of *Crimewatch* slipped neatly into place.

· PARTNERS IN CRIME? *CRIMEWATCH*, THE POLICE AND PUBLIC ·

What this concern with 'law and order' politics also indicated, of course, was a shift in the nature of the public's relationship with the police. Fears that crime was spiralling out of control and the call for the public themselves to essentially 'police' their own communities, implied a certain disillusionment or loss of confidence in the police's ability to quash (what was perceived and constructed as) rising crime. Hence the relationship between the police and *Crimewatch* is an intriguing one. It is the only programme of its kind in Britain to have serving officers actually taking part as regular presenters, a commitment on their part that surely indicates the faith the police place in the programme. In a response worth quoting at length here, series producer Katie Thomson commented that *Crimewatch*'s unique relationship with the police was, in her view, a key factor in the programme's enduring popularity over and above its competitors. When I asked her how she would account for the success of *Crimewatch* she replied,

> It's popular because we get good cases, because we have the trust of the police. And that's because we've been running so long, which was hard at the start. It's taken us many years to do, we had to get over that police mistrust of the media, especially 18 years ago when it was quite a different ball game anyway. The police now know how we operate; nothing confidential has ever been leaked from the programme. What we put out are appeals that are very much created *with* them to make the best appeal points. We always get the co-operation of the police or virtually always do. So that when contenders come in – its taken us a long time to get that relationship with the police, that's kept us ahead of the game – other people who've tried to set up similar programmes have found that very difficult to do. (Thomson, 2002)

The closeness of their co-operation and interdependence, where *Crimewatch* has become 'a vital police resource' (Amelia Hill, 2001: 7), is borne out too by Nick Ross in his foreword to the most recent *Crimewatch* book; '*Crimewatch* has become an increasing part of the armoury of the police, a resource to which they can turn much as they would make use of a forensic science lab' (Ross in H. Miller, 2001: 10). But the BBC has also been at pains to stress their editorial autonomy. As Sue Cook and Nick Ross, the first presenters of the series, put it in their book about the show, an 'enduring problem has been to ensure that our professional relationship with the police does not become so embracing that it puts in jeopardy the independence of the BBC' (Ross and Cook, 1987: 156). Hence, the programme makers decided at the onset that BBC presenters would be emphasised as 'in charge' of the programme and that police officers, even those that were presenters, would be seen as 'guests' (Ross and Cook, 1987: 156). This is evident in that the police (one exceptional case being the reconstruction of *Crimewatch* presenter Jill Dando's murder, broadcast in May 1999 and on the anniversary of her death in April 2000),[3] never narrate or introduce reconstructions, but keep to the more 'minor' features/appeals, namely photos, e-fits and video footage.

In terms of address, Ross and Cook also claim to 'avoid the use of the term "we" when referring to the police' (1987). This claim to distinguish police/presenters by avoiding the use of 'we' is not borne out in the programme itself, however. The term 'we' is used so recurrently that it is difficult at times to distinguish exactly who is included in it; it arguably encompasses presenters, police, public, victims – it is only criminals who are apparently excluded from this 'we'. For example in June 2000, in the Mandy Power murder case, Nick Ross introduces the reconstruction with the words 'Twice before *we've* appealed on one of the most shocking crimes in Britain since the war. *We* promised *we'd* stay with it and here *we* are again'. The 'we' here seems to refer broadly to all on the programme. Alternatively, though, in May 2000 a series of CCTV pictures of suspects wanted for causing criminal damage is preceded in Detective Supt Jeremy Paine's introduction with the words, 'Most of us saw the footage of mayhem on May Day when the anti-capitalist demo turned to violence'. Arguably the 'us' here includes and goes beyond the programme makers and presenters, to embrace the viewer too.

Indeed, Fairclough has argued that the close interaction between police and presenters means that 'voices are not neatly associated with roles' in the programme (1995: 154). He doesn't acknowledge, though, as I indicate above, that there is a kind of hierarchy in the different sorts of appeals. The most 'prestigious' and weighty of these – reconstructions – are presented solely by the professional/civilian presenters, thus distinguishing them as such. Confirmation of their focal place in the programme is borne out by the fact that *Crimewatch*'s own unpublished audience research found that they were the most popular element of the show; 'everyone likes the reconstructions most' (Thomson, 2002). But, nevertheless, Fairclough's assertion that the 'fudging of the differences between mediators and public officials' contributes overall to 'restructuring police–public relations in a way that helps legitimize the police' (1995: 154) is accurate, as I discuss below.

Initially, though, the emergence of *Crimewatch* arguably indicated a certain ambivalence about the role of the police in this era. In some ways it could be said to have risked undermining them – it demonstrated that the police frequently relied on public support, collaboration or information where other kinds of detection failed. In their audience research into the programme, one of Schlesinger et al.'s respondents voiced this critique nicely, when she expressed her resentment towards what she saw as the lackadaisical role of police in the programme. As she put it: 'Yes, and another thing that annoyed me, the police were sitting there answering the phone. We're the ones that are supposed to be doing all the work, we're the ones that are supposed to be saying, "Right, we're giving the information; there's a name, there's an address." They don't have to do anything, just get the guy' (Schlesinger et al., 1992: 74), a comment which underlines the concern that *Crimewatch* effectively asks the public to do the police's job.

Furthermore, the emergence of *Crimewatch* also showed the police as sometimes *having* to collaborate with the media to get their job done. Though of course the police had always done this to some extent, this was an era when the police service (not 'force' as they were previously called, a revealing shift in semantics) were growing increasingly publicly accountable and hence PR conscious. They were compelled to realise that it was to their advantage to court the media rather than combat them. Palmer notes that in 1988 Wolf Olins produced *A Force for Change: Report on the Corporate Identity of the Metropolitan Police*, which examined the existing relations between the police and media. Palmer suggests, 'This began a lengthy process of change which has seen the police and the media working together more closely' (2003: 47) (see also Mawby, 2001; Leishman and Mason, 2003: 35–42). Indeed, shortly after the release of this report, writing in *The Listener* in 1989 about his concerns that the ethical ambiguities surrounding *Crimewatch* had received scant attention, Bob Woffinden argued that the programme provided a huge PR boost for the police 'at a time when their public image is in a state of dishevelment' (1989: 11). He went on to cite John Alderson, the former Chief Constable of Devon and Cornwall, as having said, 'If a creditable organisation like the BBC will play these games, it gives the police a status and credibility that is phenomenal' (Woffinden, 1989: 11).

But despite this early potential for discomfort or friction in the relationship between police and programme, in other ways, then and now, the show popularises, celebrates and embraces the police. It attempts to break down barriers between police and public, or a 'them and us' relationship, by its inscription of an ideal citizen, an imagined community and a shared fight against crime. Hence, Biressi situates *Crimewatch* within what she calls 'law and order programming', a broader televisual movement she sees emerging in the period (including *Crimestoppers* and *Crime Monthly*), engaged in discursively constructing a 'moral subject' that is 'emblematic of a particular socio-political moment in Britain' (2001: 73). She goes on,

> The programme's depiction of the consequences of inaction or lack of vigilance on the part of the individual returns the problem of crime to the private citizen rather than to the state, 'constructing a new citizenship through fear' ... These programmes exhibit no interest in the causes of crime and criminality; instead they present themselves as an instrument through which the private person ... can help the police solve specific crimes. (Biressi, 2001: 76)

In what follows I want to look now more closely at how this 'private person' is actually addressed and constructed by the programme as an active and participatory citizen-viewer.

· REINSCRIBING THE COMMUNITY IN THE FACE OF INDIVIDUALISM ·

In a kind of 'spirit of the Blitz' mentality, then, *Crimewatch* calls on all decent folk (and indeed more unsavoury folk who nevertheless still have some kind of social conscience) to do their bit and help the police. In fact, this points to one of the central paradoxes and challenges that *Crimewatch* faces: while the very existence of the programme points to the fact that traditional forms of supportive and secure communities are at best under threat and at worst lost, it is these 'communities' and belief in the resilience of community spirit that are called on for assistance. In other words, though this programme points to the fact that we now live in an age that apparently necessitates national television appeals to deal with the growth of serious and violent crime, its discourse pivots on a nostalgic evocation of community; it appeals to the very thing whose loss it decries. Indeed, Gray Cavender has noted in relation to *America's Most Wanted* and *Survivor* that reality TV promotes the ideal of community while simultaneously undermining and eroding it through anxious discourses that pivot on competitiveness, mistrust and informing (2004). *Crimewatch*'s challenge, then, is to tread the fine line between demonstrating the need for the programme – criminality is pervasive enough to make it necessary – and demonstrating that there is still sufficient community spirit left out there to make appeals to that community meaningful. Again, this balancing act engages with prevalent law and order discourses of the time. As Palmer observes, 'Another dominant trend in policy thinking in the 1980s and 1990s was to increase the involvement of the community. Under the Tories the claim was made that social disorganisation played an important part in escalating levels of crime. What was needed was for the community to reassert itself as a moral force, as "active citizens"' (2003: 72).

In fact, we might say that *Crimewatch* helps manufacture a postmodern or non-traditional kind of community, a larger, national, *television* community that exists above and beyond many regional or cultural frontiers. The viewer may or may not belong to their own local community, but when they tune in they become part of what Rath has called 'the invisible electronic network'. Through this process 'isolated homes and dwellings' become linked to one another at the moment they turn on their televisions (Rath, 1985: 200), (though Schlesinger and Tumber have rightly warned against the vision of an entirely homogeneous and compliant audience that this conceptualisation might be said to infer (1993: 20)). Interestingly, the network imagined by Rath presages the way *America's Most Wanted* (*AMW*) describes itself over 10 years later. As Margaret Derosia describes, on 18 July 1998, the tenth anniversary episode of the programme was introduced by presenter John Walsh with the words, 'Ten years ago, we decided to use television as a nationwide crime-fighting tool, to deputize everyone in America as members of an *electronic, interactive posse'* (2002: 237; my italics). Walsh's language here also takes on a nationalist slant characteristic of the programme, potently merging the pioneer spirit and rhetoric of the US historical West with discourses drawn from contemporary technology.

More recently, the website for *America's Most Wanted* – amw.com – utilising the internet's technological potential for audience/'community'/text interactivity in ways that were still unimagined when Rath was writing, is particularly interesting in this respect. Beyond watching the show, beyond the remote possibility of making a call, interested viewers can opt to become a member of amw.com. The *Crimewatch* website is, arguably, more informative than 'interactive', though one can of course submit information regarding appeals by email. But on amw.com, the services that members can sign up for include a weekly newsletter and updates such as 'news breaks', 'capture flash', 'missing report'. One can search previous shows; look for fugitives by geography or name; or examine the FBI and US Marshals' Most Wanted lists, in addition to the 'AMW Dirty Dozen' ('the 12 fugitives John Walsh wants to take off the streets the most'). Discussion boards allow participants to discuss the programme as well as other crime issues; one can watch video clips of fugitives on '15 Seconds of Shame'; and 'Breaking Stories' may even appear while one is online. In August 2005 the site promised that merchandise would soon be available, with the 'AMW Gear' online store due to launch shortly. In other words, for the dedicated viewer using the website, *America's Most Wanted* exists above and beyond television and very much addresses and constructs a community of viewer-citizens presumed to be regular, active 'participants'. Equally, too the programme constructs a community in a more traditional, nationalist sense: the show's slogan – '*America's Most Wanted* – Where America Fights Back' both speaks of its rather more belligerent discourses regarding criminality and its patriotic appeal to active citizenry.

In television crime appeal programming the viewer is always addressed as an integral part of the appeal process. *Crimewatch* repeatedly reminds its audience or 'network' not just of its duty to get involved but of the value of that involvement. Even the announcer introducing the show before the credits joins this mode of address: 'Your call counts now on *Crimewatch UK* ...'. Throughout the show we are pleaded with ('Please don't turn your back on these crimes ... with your help we can do something about it'); reminded ('We're live as always ... waiting to take your call'), praised ('Fantastic results last month, it takes just one call to the programme to make a difference') and cajoled ('You might be able to earn yourself a reward') over our role in the show and, by extension, in crime reduction and justice. *Crimewatch* series producer Katie Thomson commented that it was exactly this spirit of community that had prompted them to introduce the 'Your Call Counts' updates,

> That's why we've got Your Call Counts.[4] Because I'm very conscious that you're giving everyone this diet of crime. In 'Your Call Counts', we say, 'This is how you solved crime', we say, 'It's not the programme that solved it, you as viewers have solved it'. And we're very conscious of it. It's really important that people feel involved. (2002)

Examining the reality TV phenomena in the US, Bill Nichols similarly identifies a common generic mode of address that calls on the audience to take an active part and see themselves as part of a larger social group being appealed to. His position is far more explicit than Rath's, however, as he takes a stance of dismay and condemnation against the form, seeing it as a genre cynically and fraudulently feigning social concern to conceal its real aim of sustaining consumption; 'Social responsibility dissolves into tele-participation. Our subjectivity is less that of citizens, social actors or "people" than of cyborg collaborators in the construction of a screen-world whose survival hinges on a support system designed to jack us into the surrounding commodity stream' (Nichols, 1994: 54). For Nichols, the genre's 'community' can only exist at the level of simulacra. Yet Annette Hill suggests that the agenda of some reality TV programming can be linked back to that of pioneer documentary filmmaker John Grierson, who saw documentary as a tool that could be used 'to promote citizenship and social responsibility' (Annette Hill, 2000: 230). Though clearly there are many marked differences between reality programming and Griersonian documentary, the public service address of *Crimewatch* does indeed seem to form parallels with Grierson's vision of documentary as a community-building tool.

Interestingly, *Crimewatch*'s evocation of an ideal community and its relationship with law and order in some ways recalls another British icon of TV crime, *Dixon of Dock Green* (BBC, 1955–78). The show was one of British television's earliest and most successful forays into crime drama and its visibility and popularity were such that it soon became part of the national consciousness. Early series were introduced with a trademark 'Evening all' from the archetypal friendly 'bobby on the beat' George Dixon and framed by his opening and closing monologues that reflected on the moral implications of the story, 'a tidy summary with some *bons mots* to encourage the belief that justice is always served' – a style which eventually came to be perceived as an irritatingly 'condescending address' (Cashmore, 1994: 156). The same kind of parochial concern and reassurance can be found in Nick Ross's image as 'the caring, sharing face of the nineties' (Paterson, 1994: 11), a man with a 'burning social conscience' (Green, 1994: 31). Ross's persona marks him as someone who cares passionately about crime both on-screen and off – his volunteer work has included membership of the Council of Victim Support and the National Crime Prevention Board (Culf, 1993: 9) and he was instrumental in establishing the Jill Dando Institute of Crime Science at University College, London. (Indeed, in Chapter 2 we shall see how the programme's producers credit Ross as having been a key asset in the programme's success).

The same aura of dedication is true of John Walsh, the presenter of *America's Most Wanted*, albeit due to a rather more serious and tragic set of circumstances. Until 1981, amw.com explains, he used to run a 'successful hotel management co. He and his wife Revé were living the American dream'. Then his six-year-old son Adam was abducted from a suburban shopping mall. The child's body was later discovered 100 miles away, and no-one was ever charged or convicted of the murder – the key suspect died in prison. Walsh's profile on the website tells us, 'The Walsh's [sic] turned their grief in to action and without a badge or a gun, John Walsh quickly became a nationally recognised leader in the push for victim's [sic] rights'. In the 1980s he was instrumental in creating The National Center for Missing and Exploited Children in the USA and he is the only private person ever to have received a Special Recognition Award from the US Attorney General. Noting how successful Walsh had been in his campaigning and realising how he was uniquely placed to bring a degree of poignancy and credibility to the role, in 1987 Fox contacted him asking him to host their new crime appeal show *America's Most Wanted*. 'Using AMW as his vehicle for justice, John could now bring to other victims of violent crime the closure he never found' (www.amw. com). Such has been Walsh's subsequent popularity that he hosted *The John Walsh Show*, his own (albeit short-lived) daytime talk show with a crime bent for a period (NBC, 2002–3) and amw.com includes a hyperlink where one can request his autograph. Again, then, Walsh's persona carries a heightened sense of commitment to the values of the programme; he speaks to the audience as someone from the community whom circumstances transformed into a 'celebrity', a victim of crime, but also a survivor. His regular sign-off – 'You *can* make a difference' – is all the more resonant for his personal history.

Ross too has his own distinctive 'catch-phrase', an optimistic sign-off like Dixon of Dock Green's moral summary, which underlines some of the programmes' shared outlook despite their different generic roots (i.e. crime fiction *vs* real crime). He reminds the audience at the end of every show that the kinds of crime featured are rare, so 'Don't have nightmares. Do sleep well'. Just as Jack Warner, the actor who played Dixon, starred in the programme from its inception, Ross, too, has been with *Crimewatch* since the first broadcast. Like Dixon, his opening remarks (made with his female co-presenter) and 'afterword' always 'frame' the proceedings, marking both him and the format of the programme as reassuringly constant and familiar. But like Dixon too, these efforts at paternal reassurance can backfire: Ross's catch-phrase sign-off has been criticised for being trite and patronising (see Schlesinger et al., 1992: 69). In Alan Clarke's words, Dixon had a 'sense of community which informed concern about crime, represented as a neighbourly interest in something which could affect each and every one of the audience' and a 'spirit of co-operation and optimism' (1992: 237). Much the same could be said of the spirit of *Crimewatch*'s mode of address.

In different ways *Crimewatch* attempts to diffuse the paradox, to bridge the gap between the imagined, nostalgic *community* it still desires and the modern 'stakeholders society', characterised by *individual* responsibility, in which it is made. It suggests both that it is the individual's responsibility to defend the law and the community and that the aspirations of today's conscientious citizens are really no different to those of the good folk and communities of yesteryear. For example, in the January 2000 edition Detective Supt Jeremy Paine introduced CCTV footage of a building-society robbery in Southport with the commentary; 'When I was growing up people pulled back the net curtains. Nowadays we have close circuit cameras instead'. This remark is interesting firstly for its use of direct address. Direct address is crucial to the programme in terms of its sense of intimacy with the viewer and its sense of liveness (as I discuss further in Chapter 3). In his use of the first person singular and in making a kind of anecdotal aside, Paine breaks down barriers between himself and the audience; he may be a policeman but he is prepared to give a little of 'himself' away in this remark. He is an ordinary man, he seems to want to tell us; he grew up with net curtains and nosy neighbours. There is an inscription of everydayness in this detail that makes him familiar to us, not 'other'. Furthermore, his observation suggests there is really no difference between old-fashioned nosy neighbours and CCTV; this new technology simply perpetuates the principles of good neighbourliness and community spirit by keeping a watchful eye on those up to no good. The essential difference in human agency is downplayed since the success of the technology *depends* on human agency; the pictures are no use if people don't call to identify the criminals. The tools may have changed, then, but the necessity of community spirit hasn't. In a similar vein, in May 2000 Nick Ross invokes personal experience while issuing a warning about a fax scam doing the rounds. Victims have been conned into giving away their bank details after receiving a fax asking for help in transferring money out of West Africa; predictably their own accounts have then been emptied. Ross warns, 'Anyone can be approached. In fact this one was sent to my own office last week', as he holds a piece of paper aloft. In adding this personal touch, evidence of how he himself has been touched by criminal endeavours, he foregrounds how he is involved not just as presenter of *Crimewatch*, but as an ordinary, potential victim ('Anyone can be approached') like any of us. As law-abiding citizens we are 'in it together' in the fight against crime, and we must look out for one another together.

In his community, 'Dixon and his colleagues were partners with the public' (Cashmore, 1994: 156) and again *Crimewatch* seeks to promote this sense of partnership. For example, in a 'Your Call Counts' section of the February 2000 edition, presenter Fiona Bruce interviews the mother of a kidnapped baby, now safely returned, and the officer in charge of the case, Chief Supt Stuart Hyde. Bruce asks, 'And, Stuart, how helpful were the local community?' He replies that they were very helpful and adds, 'But I think we've got to say a big thank you to *Crimewatch*'. Bruce signs off smiling saying 'That's fantastic. We all really cared about his case and we weren't going to let it drop'. (Note the use of the inclusive 'we' again.) However, as Clarke also notes, given the social changes that had occurred during the life-span of *Dixon of Dock Green* and the shifts towards violence and action in televisual style that had become apparent in other TV crime series, by the time of the mid-1970s and the programme's demise 'it became increasingly clear that Dixon was a product of a world that was in the process of ceasing to exist' (Clarke, 1992: 241). It is this lost or endangered world, characterised by community, responsibility and integrity, that *Crimewatch* aspires to or indeed seeks to revive. Each time one of the presenters uses the term 'we' they flatter the viewer by aligning themselves with them and symbolically assume their incorporation into *Crimewatch*'s televisual crime-fighting community. This inscribes a kind of intimacy and familiarity that is characteristic of what John Ellis has called TV's 'community of address'. But where there is a 'we' there must also, by inference, be a 'they'. This mode of address means, then, that,

> The distance between viewer and image is reduced; but a compensatory distance is constructed and separation/between the 'I' and 'you' of the community of address and the third person outside that it constructs. The 'they' that is always implied and often stated in direct address forms becomes an other, a

> grouping outside the consensus that confirms the consensus. (Ellis, 1994: 139)

Ellis describes television's construction of 'the black community' and 'housewives' as pre-eminent examples of TV's capacity to construct groups of 'others'. In Chapter 5 I make a detailed analysis of *Crimewatch*'s representation of women in its reconstructions. But for a moment here I want to reflect on how *Crimewatch* deals with, or diffuses, the 'problem' of a disenfranchised or 'other' group in relation to its representation of two highly charged cases of racist murder.[5]

The community as imagined by *Crimewatch,* then, is a triumvirate of police, programme and public. The January and March 2000 episodes show the extent to which the programme seeks to demonstrate this as a mutually supportive triumvirate in action. These episodes dealt with two separate cases of high-profile and controversial racist murders of young black men and featured an interview with one of the Metropolitan Police's highest-ranking officers at that time, Deputy Assistant Commissioner John Grieve, who headed the Race and Violent Crimes Taskforce at the Met in this period. In January, Grieve appeared in a 'Your Call Counts' section of the show following the successful conviction of two men responsible for the murder of Michael Menson, a murder that had initially been mistakenly treated as a suicide. While discussing their success in bringing these murderers to justice, Grieve reveals he will be back soon to discuss developments in another (unsolved) racist murder, that of Stephen Lawrence. This high-profile inquiry was a notoriously badly managed investigation that famously led to the Metropolitan Police being accused of 'institutionalised racism' by an inquiry into the case's mismanagement (the Macpherson Report).[6] Rather than stress the need for public help by alluding to the shortcomings of the police in these cases, which might of course endanger police co-operation, references to police corruption or mismanagement are overwhelmingly absent. Ross and Grieve discuss the Menson case in the following way:

> *NR:* John, you've gone out of your way to praise the role of *Crimewatch* in this but actually the truth is there was extremely good police work on your part among others and of

course the most important thing is the pivotal role of the family themselves.

JG: Yes, you're right Nick, the family were utterly pivotal ... but
if they were pivotal it was *Crimewatch* who levered open the
witnesses for us, that led us to the people who knew about the
conspiracy and helped the police. ... This was a good example
of the family and *Crimewatch* appealing to people to do their
public duty. That's what broke this case.

This exchange appeals to a sense of community, duty and family.
References to the family are actually extremely euphemistic – in
fact, in conflict with the police, Menson's family had complained
about police mismanagement of the case and campaigned for his
death to be investigated as a murder inquiry. Ross and Grieve's
words, though, are mutually self-congratulatory; they swap
endorsements of one another to show the police and *Crimewatch*
as a united front, full of mutual admiration. The cosy familiarity
of the exchange of first names between the presenter and senior
police officer suggests a warm camaraderie. John Grieve goes on
to promise to come back again soon for help on the Stephen Lawrence case, like a popular guest on a chat show. Though it has
clearly never been *Crimewatch*'s aim or purpose to discuss policing
policy, all in all this exchange looks suspiciously like a PR exercise
dressed as an 'exclusive'. It would doubtlessly ring alarm bells for
those critics who have expressed fears that crime reconstructions
necessitate programme makers' reliance on the police for material, thereby compromising their impartiality and integrity.[7]
Given the high-profile nature of the Stephen Lawrence case, and
the fact that following the inquiry into this case Grieve was
appointed to his role to appease public fears that racist attacks
were not dealt with by the Met Police with sufficient gravity, this
exchange seems highly stage-managed. It appears to want to link
Grieve and the solving of one racist murder positively to developments in the Stephen Lawrence case – as if by association, the
successful outcome of the Menson case may rub off on the Lawrence one – deflecting attention away from the fact that both
investigations were accused of racism and mismanagement and
there were never any convictions regarding the latter.

In fairness, however, other controversial cases are covered
more frankly in other programmes. For example, in the Telford

Hangings case dealt with in June 2000 Ross interviews the brother of one of the victims and acknowledges how, again, the suspicious deaths of two black men were initially treated as suicides by police, asking pointedly, 'What are relations like with the police, because they were pretty bad at one stage, you thought the police had made a real mess of investigations?' More recently, the suspected Loyalist murder of Sean Brown in Northern Ireland in 1997 was reconstructed in the June 2005 edition of the programme. The shoddy and controversial handling of the case by the initial investigators is openly acknowledged by Ross when he introduces the reconstruction, noting that the Royal Ulster Constabulary had been in charge of the investigation: 'But mistakes were made, evidence was overlooked, important documents disappeared. An independent review damned the investigation's failures. The job had not been properly done. Eight years on a new team of detectives has started again from scratch'.

Also, in 2001 Nick Ross hit the headlines for criticising the 'kneejerk reactions' of government and police crime policy. In an 'outspoken' interview in the *Observer* he criticised the reactive nature of policing method in the UK and Prime Minister Tony Blair's famous 'soundbite' on Labour's crime policy, asking, 'But where is our great strategy with crime? It's all rhetoric. "Tough on crime, tough on the causes of crime"? – it's meaningless garbage' (Amelia Hill, 2001: 7). It was not so much the content of the interview, but the fact that *Ross*, 'the high-profile presenter of the BBC's *Crimewatch* programme' (Amelia Hill, 2001: 7) was saying it, which made his comments news. This demonstrates again the potent place *Crimewatch* holds in the British public's perception of crime; his comments became controversial because in the interview Ross apparently 'breaks ranks' with the generally affirmative address of the programme to criticise rather than endorse policy. The story also underlines something again about Ross's persona; his speaking out so forthrightly suggests again the utter and genuine commitment he has to truly tackling crime. In fact, the interview also appears to have been timed to correspond with the publication of the second *Crimewatch* book in 2001, *Crimewatch Solved – The Inside Story* by Hugh Miller, for which Ross wrote the foreword. In the final page of his comments, Ross actually appears to critique the programme's remit for contributing to

a political and social climate that is more concerned with apprehending criminals than reducing crime,

> Actually, though you may be surprised to hear this, I have
> become increasingly aware that what we do on *Crimewatch*, and
> what police and lawyers do, is often tangential to crime, a dis-
> traction from other fundamentals. Of course it is important to
> catch offenders; it is also right to target a national TV appeal at
> the most serious crimes rather than, for example, a local bur-
> glary. But too much emphasis is on shutting the stable door after
> the horses have bolted, and too little attention is spent on for-
> mal crime reduction. (Ross in H. Miller, 2001: 16)

Nevertheless, discordant moments *within the programme* that
engage with criticisms of the police are rare and, even in the Telford Hangings and Sean Brown cases above, are quickly passed
over. The narrow range of perspectives on crime that *Crimewatch*
actually engages with – a deficiency that Nick Ross himself
criticises above – would in part be addressed by a greater contextualisation of crime at times. Like the programme's refusal, for
example, to acknowledge the preponderance of domestic violence over stranger attacks as by far and away the form of violence
most likely to effect women (see Chapter 5), this smoothing over
of allegations of racism in the police is another way in which it
can be said that *Crimewatch* avoids explicitly engaging with contentious political and social issues that are inextricably bound up
in both the occurrence and representation of crime. The focus is
exclusively on criminal capture, not the 'causes of crime', nor the
aftermath of conviction. Furthermore, as Schlesinger and Tumber
have observed, 'It poses no difficult questions about the effective-
ness of the police nor about their methods in achieving results,
although these have become major issues of public concern'
(1993: 22). In fact, Hill has suggested that this reluctance to
engage with broader cultural contexts is characteristic of the
wider emergency services based reality TV movement, demonstrating again how selective any version of 'real life' inevitably is
and how not all 'facts' are of equal interest to these 'factual' programmes. On *999*, *Blues and Twos* and *Coppers* she writes, 'What is
absent from these reality programmes is the "real" story of Britain's emergency services. The economic and recruitment

problems of the NHS, or the evidence of racism and corruption in the Metropolitan Police, are not part of the agenda of reality programmes' (Annette Hill, 2000: 231).

In this chapter, then, we have seen how *Crimewatch* can be understood as emerging during a significant transitional moment in British society's relationship with the police and popular conceptualisations of crime and approaches to crime reduction. In this way it provides a rich case study for thinking about the ways in which real crime TV, and popular television generally, both reflects or responds to the cultural preoccupations of its times and plays a part in diffusing and attenuating those preoccupations. Close textual analysis reveals how *Crimewatch* has nurtured both an intimate relationship with the police and a mode of address that pivots on a nostalgic and reaffirming appeal to community – a concept that is perceived as under threat in this era. These characteristics are fundamental components in its identity and mark it as largely conservative in its operation; a programme that seeks to evoke and maintain a consensus culture rather than to explore the factors that underlie any alleged demise in community or shifts in the incidence of crime generally believed to have occurred in Britain during the last two decades. However, despite its apparent efforts at deflecting attention away from serious social debate through a focus on its own tangible results, in the next chapter I examine how *Crimewatch* and real crime programming as a whole became a contentious subject of debate themselves in the 1980s/90s 'fear-of-crime' panic.

· NOTES ·

1 This point was made to me in an informal discussion with Crimestoppers detectives at New Scotland Yard in 1994.
2 www.bbc.co.uk/crime/crimewatch, accessed 13 July 2005.
3 On 26 April 1999, Jill Dando, who co-presented *Crimewatch* with Nick Ross at this time, was shot and killed on the doorstep of her home in London. An allegedly obsessed fan, Barry George, was later convicted of her murder. For a full discussion of the British media's coverage of her murder, see Jermyn (2001). Dando was replaced on the programme by Fiona Bruce.

4　At the time of interview, the 'Your Call Counts' updates, regarding previous crimes covered on the programme, were signalled by their own graphic insert. These graphics have since been dropped but the updates are still very much an integral part of the programme.

5　For a discussion of race and racism in *America's Most Wanted*, see Derosia, 2002.

6　It is interesting in this respect to note that in 2004, as if to assist the police in their efforts to project a more ethnically diverse image, *Crimewatch* recruited PCs Jonathan Morrison and Rav Wilding as 'the programme's first black and Asian presenters' (www.bbc.co.uk/crime/crimewatch/ravjonathan, accessed 13 July 2005).

7　See for example Richard Ingrams (1994) who writes 'it is simply not the job of the BBC to act as a willing arm of the law enforcement process'.

2 From 'Public Service' to 'Fear of Crime'

TELEVISION, ANXIETY AND CRIME APPEAL PROGRAMMING

The many troubling paradoxes and contradictions that haunt *Crimewatch* are unsurprising, perhaps, given the inherently contentious and disquieting nature of its essential project; that is, to enlist the public via national prime-time TV to assist the police in solving crimes across the country. Even from this briefest synopsis of the programme's remit a number of challenges and issues emerge. It points to the loaded terms that we shall see recur throughout discourses surrounding *Crimewatch,* focusing on accountability and editorial control (is this the BBC's show or the police's?); creative licence versus authenticity (when the full facts aren't known what are the ethical problems with filling in the 'gaps'?); 'good taste' versus exploitation (outside the news and documentary, should real crime and human suffering become the stuff of prime-time?); and the question of just what kind of programming this is ('mini-drama-documentary' (Palmer, 2003: 79); 'infotainment' (Leishman and Mason, 2003: 113; Annette Hill, 2005: 26) or 'collaborational' (Kilborn, 2003: 68)?). Despite these troubling grey areas, as we have seen, the programme has outlived both its critics and competitors, defending itself on the grounds of its public service function and impressive results. As the BBC's deputy head of features, Anne Morrison, put it in 1992: '*Crimewatch* takes seriously our mission to help the police solve serious crime. Our reconstructions concentrate on clues which may jog someone's memory and avoid sensationalising the crimes. So far,

320 arrests and 184 convictions have resulted directly from the programme' (Morrison, 1992: 20).

Similarly, series producer Katie Thomson commented that in her view, 'People feel it is, in the purest sense, public service broadcasting, in that we're giving out information that could help solve a murder or rape, to ask the public to help with. It doesn't come much clearer than that really, in that the public is needed above and beyond the needs of television' (2002). In this summation of public service broadcasting, the role and participation of *the viewer* is what is most valued. It is actually more important than the medium; television is simply the means to an end. She goes on,

> Because it's not about television anymore, it becomes about something that's bigger than television. Television's so transient but *Crimewatch* isn't a transient programme. It's something that after we go off air, the repercussions rumble on for months or even years. That's the huge, sort of power of television, but actually it's the power of the viewer. Because *Crimewatch* doesn't exist without the viewer. I know programmes wouldn't exist if people didn't watch them but this is slightly different in that *Crimewatch*'s whole *raison d'être* is that people have to watch it. (Thomson, 2002)

Nevertheless, despite the vision of *Crimewatch*'s worthy project and an empowered audience evoked by Thomson here, one of the most enduring critiques of the show has been its role in promoting the 'fear of crime'. For example, in February 2003, in his review of the controversial French film *Irreversible* (dir. Noe, 2002), Nick James directly compares the film to *Crimewatch* for the way in which it 'plays on fear of the streets'. Like *Crimewatch*, he says, it 'feed[s] urban paranoia' (James, 2003: 21). The easy invoking of this *British television* text to make a point about a *French film* underlines the extent to which both the programme, and this critique of it, are part of Britain's popular consciousness.

The issue of fear of crime was making its way firmly onto Britain's social agenda at exactly the point that *Crimewatch* first appeared; the second British Crime Survey in 1984 differed from the first in 1981 in that 'A significant new line of enquiry included in this survey was the degree to which respondents were afraid or anxious about crime' (Gunter, 1987: 2). Its memorable findings included the fact that 31% of respondents felt 'fairly unsafe' or 'very unsafe' walking around after dark in their own neighbourhood (Gunter, 1987: 3). One can see, then, how the growing awareness of fear of crime was bound up in the perception that notions of community were fracturing. At the same time, there was a notable rise in crime programming on British television screens. Though *Police 5* ran for 30 years, it was really the advent of *Crimewatch* in 1984 and its subsequent success that later gave rise to a flurry of similar programmes dramatising or reconstructing 'real' crimes, some already alluded to here, such as *Crimestoppers, Crime Monthly, Crime Stalker* (ITV, 1993–7), *Crime Limited* (BBC, 1992–4) *Michael Winner's True Crimes* (ITV, 1991–4) and *In Suspicious Circumstances* (Carlton, 1994–5). It wasn't long before the two trends were linked. From the late 1980s through to the mid-1990s particularly, the preponderance of such programmes and their grim fascination with recounting criminal activity came under regular fire from interested groups and the media itself for the damage they were apparently wreaking on national morale. The popularisation of 'real crime' as the focus for so many shows, be they motivated predominantly by entertainment, crime prevention, appeals for information or some mix of all the above, was thought to be contributing to a climate where the public perception of crime levels was becoming wildly distorted. Rather than alleviating criminal activity, these programmes were whipping up the fear of crime. Hence, in this chapter I seek to contextualise *Crimewatch* further by situating it within the potent fear-of-crime debates that raged around British television and its representation of crime in the 1980s and early 1990s, as other real crime programmes also started to appear in considerable numbers. This is pursued partly through a comparative analysis of *Crimewatch* and the UK's other leading television crime appeal programmes since its advent – namely *Crime Monthly* and *Britain's Most Wanted* – which are examined in terms of their distinctiveness from *Crimewatch* and some of the wider issues raised by these programmes' different public service and commercial broadcasting roots.

· THE WAGES OF 'HEAVY' VIEWING ·

Concerns about television's power to distort people's perception of the world – suggesting that the more television one viewed the more likely one was to see the world as a violent place – had been in circulation for some time already by this period. They had been raised most famously perhaps by George Gerbner and Larry Gross in their 1976 US research study, 'Living with Television: The Violence Profile'. This research argued that the function of television was 'in a word, enculturation' (Gerbner and Gross, 1976: 175). Through the methodological approach of 'cultivation analysis' they sought to identify 'the assumptions television cultivates about the facts, norms and values of society' (Gerbner and Gross, 1976: 182). They found that the world of television drama heavily over-played the prevalence of violence in comparison to its incidence in the 'real' world, but that television cultivated its own reality. 'Heavy' television viewers were more likely to exhibit general distrust towards strangers and to overestimate substantially the likelihood of their being involved in violence (Gerbner and Gross, 1976: 192–3). They concluded that, 'Television and other media exposure may be as important as demographic and other experiential factors in explaining why people view the world as they do' (Gerbner and Gross, 1976: 193). The repercussion of this heightened sense of insecurity was that (some) people were more likely to endorse or rely on forms of social and/or forceful control so that, ultimately, television's function was to operate as a socially repressive and conservative apparatus.

Gerbner and Gross's findings clearly contributed to the concerns about the ramifications of television's contribution to fear-of-crime in Britain in this period. This is despite the fact that their methodology and interpretation of their findings came in for some criticism. For example, Hughes (1980) argued that the study had failed to conceptualise adequately, and introduce controls regarding, the impact and significance of other variables – such as race, hours worked and church attendance – in the relationship between television viewing and social perceptions. On reanalysing Gerbner and Gross's material and taking these variables into account, Hughes was able to interpret the material in ways that directly contradicted some of their conclusions, 'indicating that those individuals who claimed to watch television heavily were *less* likely to be afraid of walking alone at night in the neighbourhood' (Gunter, 1987: 24). Hirsch (1980) also questioned ambiguities in Gerbner's data and argued that its categorisation of viewing behaviour into 'heavy' and 'light' models was selective and arbitrary. Gerbner and Gross did provide counter-responses to these criticisms but nevertheless the discursive forum that evolved from the research and the different interpretations made of the same raw data indicated the complexity of the issues at stake.

Furthermore, other research carried out in Britain shortly afterwards argued that the influence of television on public perceptions and fear of crime was not particularly strong. Gunter writes, 'Efforts to replicate Gerbner's findings among British samples in the late 1970s failed' (1987: 67) and attention shifted to why the US and UK contexts may have yielded different results; 'If much peak-time programming in the two countries is of a similar range of types, however, this specificity of effects may be a function of US society itself or perhaps of the way television fits into that society rather than just of the nature of what is shown on television' (1987: 69). Gunter's own 1986 audience study about television viewing and fear of crime among London residents identified the significance of a cyclical phenomenon whereby those who have the highest levels of anxiety about their safety are more likely to stay indoors (1987: 88). These viewers may then end up watching more television, where they view programmes in a manner that uses the programmes to reinforce and confirm the validity of their anxieties. Though heavy viewing was, then, a statistical predictor of fear, this viewing habit was an *effect* rather than a cause of that fear. Other research found that viewers who were apprehensive about crime would incline towards crime drama with a 'just' resolution, and that such programming then served to actually *reassure* them (Walkshag et al., cited in Sparks, 1992: 94). The 'selective exposure' theory put forward by Gunter and others has come in for criticism from Sparks, however, who has argued that, like the 'cultivation analysis' school of thought that it seeks to problematise and address, it relies on 'poorly defended interpretations of television content' (1992: 98).

Overall, then, the fear-of-crime debate has proved massively controversial within criminology and inter-disciplinary work across media studies and criminology. In addition, the differences outlined in the research above have all been haunted by the semantics and subjectivity of the terms involved. How does one deem at which point a fear is 'irrational'? Furthermore, the disjuncture between apparently objective 'real' levels of risk and 'undue' fearfulness should not lead to the assumption that such fear is therefore 'irrational' (Sparks, 1992: 7). Rather it may indicate an engagement with a whole range of other less immediately tangible risks and anxieties than those that can be measured by crime statistics. In Tulloch's words, 'Fear is not simply a quantity to be measured. It is rather, a mode of perception which is constitutive of personal identity' (2000: 188). Furthermore, just as 'irrational' is a subjective and judgement-laden term, so too is 'fear' equally nebulous. 'Fear' may manifest itself in different ways and have different prompts, meanings and ramifications for the individual, according to a variety of factors including personal experience, age, sex, race, habitat and so on:

> The problems of fear not only always involves difficult and often obscure kinds of empirical evidence but also commits the observer to making certain kinds of judgements about the appropriateness of cognitions and emotions … 'Fear' is thus a more open-textured and debatable theoretical construct than many criminologists seem ready to admit. (Sparks, 1992: 7)

Despite the evident uncertainties and contradictions that these various studies uncovered about the relationship between fear of crime and television viewing, the media were unsurprisingly drawn to the possibility that television depictions of crime were resulting in a nation consumed by isolation and fear. In sum, the possibility of a link between watching 'too much' television and experiencing paranoia about crime amounted to another episode in the 'media effects' debate (see Barker and Petley, 1994; Brooker and Jermyn, 2002). Such stories have proved enduringly attractive to journalists, who realise the inflammatory power these tales hold (or can be depicted to hold) in the public imagination; consequently something of a moral panic ensued.

Mirroring aspects of the fear-of-crime debate, with its anxiety about the 'effects' of television on its ('vulnerable') audience, was the concern that the programme might also form a prompt for *copycat* crime. However, one might equally argue that copycat crime is a form of engagement with the programme that actually demonstrates the audience as being active and discerning in the ways they 'use' the show. It also gives weight to Schlesinger and Tumber's (1993: 20) misgivings about Rath's (1985) belief in the television crime appeal's capacity to create a compliant audience, an 'invisible network' of surveillance; copycat criminals are just one example of an 'un-co-operative' audience. The potential for copycat crime was described in the BBC's audience research as an area giving rise to 'ambivalence', where in all the focus groups at least some of the respondents raised concerns that people could get information regarding 'ideas or help on how to commit a crime (and even the idea of committing a crime in the first place); on the mistakes others have made; on how to avoid the police and overcome various crime prevention methods' (BBC, 1988: 22). Respondents suggested that more attention to successful inquiries was needed to underline the likelihood of apprehension, but noted that, in the programme's defence, it was not alone in 'giving out ideas' on television. Indeed, they felt it showed restraint in revealing the details of crimes and, on balance, felt it did more to combat crime than inspire it. Copycat crime was also addressed by Ross and Cook in their book of the show, where they conclude that the potential for this use is a risk that has to be taken:

> The moral doubts were the hardest ones to answer in advance ... Might it tempt honest viewers into crime by highlighting the truth that some crimes make people rich and some are hard to solve? Might *Crimewatch* give new ideas to already dishonest people by revealing the techniques of other criminals? ... The straight answer was yes ... Of course detailed reconstructions, however sensitively done, would always introduce corrupt methods to innocent minds ... Yet any reporting of crime (or of open courts and open justice) shoulders all those dangers. (1987: 155)

The 'copycatting' critique is one that has emerged periodically throughout the programme's history. For example, in July 2000 criminologist Martin Gill's study of 341 robbers and raiders in prison appeared to bear out Ross and Cook's fears: 'Jailed bandits say the crime-fighting television show ... gave them ideas for raids and showed them how easy it was. They said bank staff on the programme rarely resist and the quality of security film was so poor suspects were difficult to identify' (Burrell, 2000). Crucially, though, Gill's findings do not just demonstrate the legitimacy of the 'media effects' debate. They also demonstrate how access to the 'realism' of genuine robberies via CCTV footage can actually be appropriated in different ways by audiences. In fact, CCTV is appropriated here in a manner *counter-productive* to *Crimewatch*'s intentions, undermining the programme's aims of criminal deterrence and identification, as it is used instead to confirm the dubious quality of some video footage and the relative ease and anonymity with which some robberies occur. CCTV here is not perceived, by the criminal audience at least, as an imposing deterrent. Rather, these respondents reflect on the use of CCTV footage as exposing its inadequacies.

Contributing to the anxious climate that surrounded discussion of real crime TV and fear of crime in this period, there were also concerns about the perceived (lack of) quality in this emergent kind of 'cheap, lazy television' (Graham, 1994: 13). These more evaluative kinds of criticism were obviously linked to the fear-of-crime debate but also independent from it to some degree, emanating from contemporary anxieties about broader shifts in Britain's changing televisual landscape. The increasing deregulation of British television at this time led to a climate of nervousness that the genre 'could be laying the ground for a new breed of American-style shows in which the distinction between fact and fiction becomes increasingly blurred' (Minogue, 1990: 23). In fact, the unease expressed in this last comment, regarding the programmes' perceived conflation of reality and fiction, was a recurrent concern, one I return to question further in the final chapter.

Of the examples of crime series given above, only *Crimewatch* still remains. Most of the others were quietly withdrawn, but the axing of *Michael Winner's True Crimes* in August 1994 'on the grounds of taste' (Campbell, 1994b: 13) very publicly and controversially crystallised the concerns and anxieties about this TV genre. Widely accused of being exploitative, *True Crimes*, which had enjoyed audiences of 10 million, featured the gregarious, outspoken film director-turned-celebrity introducing reconstructions of serious crimes in a manner rather reminiscent of *Alfred Hitchcock Presents*. Winner's monologues framed the programme, introducing the reconstruction at the start and returning for the closing epilogue with some concluding observations, as well as providing an explanatory voiceover throughout. Production values were evidently not particularly high, while the inevitably high turnover of actors meant quality performances were not assured. In the episode reconstructing the kidnap of 32-year-old Victor Cracknell, the son of a millionaire food broker (tx 27 March 1994) the programme opens with Winner sitting at his desk, next to the typewriter. Drawing us in, in the manner of a storyteller, he turns to tell the audience that what we are about to see: '[Is] an extraordinary account of technique and perseverance pitched against a determined, evil man who held all the aces. And just when you think there are no more turns the improbable plot can take, real life throws up a final twist in the tale.' Minogue's fears of 'blurring', above, take on some interesting and pertinent resonances here as Winner's prologue, while adhering to familiar suspense-building techniques, moves freely between positioning the scenes that will follow as lying somewhere between fact and fiction. In his account, the true events become a 'plot' and 'real life' intervenes in the 'tale', rather than being its very substance.

Michael Grade led the attack when he accused *Michael Winner's True Crimes* of using 'real life crime for entertainment, blurring the boundaries between reality and fiction and sensationalising terrifying crime' (Connett, 1994: 7; note the concern about 'blurred boundaries' again here). A furious Winner defended the programme, claiming that the fear-of-crime critique was immaterial since the 'public were far from being terrified by the non-revelation that crime actually exists', arguing that axing the show amounted to an 'act of censorship' (Campbell, 1994a: 16). Commentators such as the *Guardian*'s crime correspondent Duncan Campbell suggested that the genre was being used as a scapegoat – 'the latest handy excuse for worries about crime' – and commented that *True Crimes* had actually been constructed in such an overtly formulaic fashion that the reconstructions appeared far removed from reality and were 'remarkably unthreatening ... In contrast, the *Crimewatch* and *Crime Limited* programmes – fine and public spirited though they may be – are much more likely to make people fearful of crime because they deal with identifiably real events and identifiably unhappy victims' (1994a: 16). *Crimewatch*'s Nick Ross had also intervened in the debate by calling Winner's programme a 'television whore', a remark he later retracted (Harrison, 1994: 3). It was within this highly fuelled and emotive climate that Winner's programme was finally withdrawn.

Six years earlier the BBC had been sufficiently concerned regarding how the public felt about the levels of violence in *Crimewatch*'s reconstructions to carry out its own research on audience responses to *Crimewatch* (BBC, 1988), while on 11 December 1989 the Home Office Standing Conference on Crime Prevention published the report from an independent working party on the fear of crime, chaired by Michael Grade, then chief executive of Channel Four. This was followed in August 1990 by an Independent Broadcasting Authority (IBA) report on 'Crime Reconstruction Programmes' (Wober and Gunter, 1990). These reports differed to some extent on the degree to which they thought the programmes they looked at did popularise the fear of crime; in the IBA report, for example, 51% of respondents felt that watching *Crimestoppers* had not made them 'more afraid of crime'. Significantly, though, in this report nearly 40% thought 'other people' would have been made more afraid by *Crimestoppers*. This is a telling statistic in that fears about the effects of TV and the media generally have been recurrently focused on doubts about the abilities of 'others' to diffuse them, a process that works to mark some groups – notably women, children, the elderly and the working class – as marginalised and vulnerable.[1] What the reports shared was a sense that 'fear of crime is a very real social problem in itself' (Wober and Gunter, 1990: 1), that crime reconstruction programmes were particularly significant in shaping the public's perception of crime and that where fear of crime was exacerbated by the programmes, women and the elderly were most likely to be those whose fears had been heightened (a crucial point I will return to in Chapter 5). Other research commissioned by the

Broadcasting Standards Council sought to investigate more precisely how *women* specifically engaged with watching violence, resulting in Schlesinger et al.'s *Women Viewing Violence* study (1992). This research, which included close analysis of responses to an episode of *Crimewatch*, concluded that the authors of the previous reports above had been neglectful of the fear-of-crime issue since they 'may not have tapped adequately into some of the complex anxieties about personal safety that we have uncovered among women' (Schlesinger et al., 1992: 46). Having looked at the characteristic terms of address adopted in the television crime appeal in Chapter 1, in what follows I look more closely at some of the aesthetic design of these programmes and how their consistently dramatic, sometimes intimidating imagery may well foster an anxious audience, even while it simultaneously seeks to reassure them.

· *CRIMEWATCH* AND ITS CRIME APPEAL COMPATRIOTS ·

In such a climate it was partly the BBC's redress to a public service broadcasting remit, pointed to in the opening of this chapter, that undoubtedly endowed its crime reconstruction programme with a greater degree of credibility and respectability among both police and public than its commercial TV counterparts ever achieved. The success of *Crimewatch* soon led to imitations or 'rival' shows. But the combination of the BBC's inbuilt historical and national 'prestige' status – and, indeed, Nick Ross's persona, as we saw in Chapter 1, as a serious and committed presenter with a grasp of 'the subtler social dimension' – meant that when the condemnation of crime reconstruction programmes reached its height in 1994, Ross 'escape[d] most of the criticism flying around' (Paterson, 1994: 11). Indeed, when I asked series producer Katie Thomson whether she thought *Crimewatch* had an identity that differentiated it from other crime appeal programmes, she pointed to Nick Ross as a pre-eminent factor in what she saw as the programme's distinctiveness; 'I think the fact that Nick's been on it for so long. I think he's very much part of it' (2002). Public discourses about the programme confirm the degree to which it is intrinsically associated with Ross. For example, an *Observer* article in which Ross criticised government and policing crime policy described *Crimewatch* as *'Ross' own* television programme' and referred to some of the cases he had *'presided over'* (my italics), telling language that very much indicates the perception of him as 'running' the programme (Amelia Hill, 2001: 7). Thomson also commented that the programme's own (unpublished) audience research carried out shortly before our interview had found that 'Nick is seen as very instrumental in the programme and very trusted. You cannot believe how interested he genuinely is ... And I think that comes over, actually' (2002).

For Thomson, there were two further key ways in which *Crimewatch* distinguishes itself from other appeal programmes. Firstly, its high degree of police co-operation and, secondly, that 'Those that are coming in tend to be a bit more tabloid or a bit more overdramatic or sensational', evoking a traditional image of the BBC as more reserved than its commercial rivals. In fact, my textual analysis argues that *Crimewatch* reconstructions quite regularly arguably overstep this admittedly subjective line to enter into the realm of the sensational, so that Thomson's sense of *Crimewatch* as less 'tabloid' than its competitors is, on occasion, hard to defend. Much more broadly, the identities of Britain's leading terrestrial television channels are now undoubtedly less distinct than was historically the case. Nevertheless, *Crimewatch* has, perhaps, managed to ride the storm of true crime debates arguably largely because its public service cachet, even in such a climate, still endows it with a greater level of gravitas and respectability than has been perceived in its ITV counterparts.

Indeed, the Broadcasting Standards Committee (BSC) has indicated that they believe they get more complaints regarding material of an ambiguously 'questionable' nature shown on the BBC than on other channels, a fact that they attribute to the higher standards people demand of the BBC.[2] This is borne out by their figures: between 1998 and the start of 2002, for example, the BSC investigated five complaints against *Crimewatch* (including complaints against trailers and *Crimewatch File*), none of which were upheld, and just one against *Britain's Most Wanted*, which was upheld.[3] The programme concerned (tx 20 November 1998) had included an item on contract killing where 'a man who admitted to having inside knowledge of the criminal world' described how to go about organising a contract and how one might dispose of a body. Despite ITV's defence that the item did not provide any information that was not already widely known and that they 'expected that it would have deterred anyone with such ideas' the BSC found it to be 'ill-judged' and the complaint was upheld (Broadcasting Standards Committee, 1999: 5). One should remember, of course, that more episodes of *Crimewatch* had been broadcast in this period, thereby giving more occasion for complaint. But the fact that no complaints against *Crimewatch* were upheld by the BSC might be said to suggest that more people complain about relatively marginal or negligible questions of taste that ultimately, to use the BSC's words, 'do not exceed acceptable boundaries', when such material is on the BBC. This would suggest that viewers are less likely to tolerate 'sensationalism' in *Crimewatch* than in similar programmes elsewhere, since they have more critical and rigorous expectations of it. (This is interesting since alternatively, given the kudos that the BBC carries, one might have expected that viewers would be more likely to accept readily that the programme is legitimately prompted by a respectable public service motive.) In interview, the producers of *Britain's Most Wanted* were very much aware of the difference these channel origins made to the tone and the mode of address adopted by them in comparison to *Crimewatch*. Series producer Tim Miller summed this up diplomatically by arguing that ITV could afford to be '*bolder*' and, like the BSC research department above, pointed to the importance of the different expectations and standards viewers bring to bear on different channels:

> I think the audience would have a different take on it as well. I think the same viewer who watched it on BBC1, if *Crimewatch* was suddenly *Most Wanted* and that went on BBC1, that same viewer might watch it on ITV and not write and complain. I think if they watched it on the BBC they would. They have different levels of expectation. They expect ITV to be racier. That's why they watch it [laughs]. (T. Miller, 2001)

Crimewatch's most directly comparable competitors have not enjoyed anything like comparable longevity; *Crime Monthly* ran for seven years until 1996 while *Britain's Most Wanted*, which ran in series of six mid-weekly episodes broadcast at 10.30pm and each lasting 30 minutes, was introduced in 1998 and last broadcast in 2000. Of course, as we've seen, all the programmes noted here have been accused at one time or another of being sensationalist, exploitative or lurid. But significantly these reservations have been particularly pronounced in the case of the LWT and ITV incarnations and this has undoubtedly contributed to their struggle to stay on the schedule.

· FROM NEWS TO NOIR – AESTHETICS IN THE TELEVISION CRIME APPEAL ·

Of course, in order to explore fully the supposed links between this kind of programming and fear of crime, we must look carefully at the aesthetic techniques adopted by these programmes and reflect on how they seek to involve, excite, or unnerve the audience. The aesthetics of *Crime Monthly* and *Britain's Most Wanted* in many ways bore more obvious relation to one another than they did to *Crimewatch*. LWT's *Crime Monthly,* which was launched in October 1989 and later became national in 1992, was a small-scale production presented from a dimly lit studio, originally by Paul Ross and later by Penny Smith. In contrast with the sincerity and conviction of Nick Ross, Paul Ross (no relation) appeared to have been chosen for his 'wide-boy' personality. Drawing again on connotations of channel identity and difference, one reviewer described Ross as being 'shiny-suited' with 'a lager commercial accent that would get short shrift from the BBC pronunciation unit' (Minogue, 1990: 23). He was perhaps meant to add a touch of 'authenticity'; a presenter who could be perceived as somehow not too far removed from the rough and tumble of the criminal underworld.

The programme's menacing credit sequence also did much to set the tone for the programme. John Ellis has pointed to the significance of title sequences to audience relationships with programming. While discussing the ordering of television around what he calls 'segmentation' he comments,

> This segmentation extends to programmes themselves, espe-
> cially the title sequences. The title sequence is in effect a
> commercial for the programme itself, and it has all the features
> of a commercial ... it is highly organised and synoptic, providing
> a kind of narrative image for its programme ... and [it] usually
> provides a highly generalised, gestural conception of the pro-
> gramme it advertises. (Ellis, 1994: 119–20)

The 'narrative image' for *Crime Monthly* is made dramatically and
potently clear in its title sequence. The sound of an echoing, distorted electric guitar accompanies a rapidly edited montage
sequence of scenes of the city at night, many evidently shot on
location at Chinatown in London's Soho. This is a location that
immediately foregrounds the authenticity of an urban space, one
which has long been evocatively associated with crime due to its
links with prostitution, gang activity and drugs. Yet there is also
something hyper-real about this space; its image has been called
on so many times as a kind of shorthand for urban degeneracy
that it has the familiarity and predictability of a stereotype. We
open with a camera zooming into the top floors of a tower block,
followed by slow motion, distorted shots of shops, buses and a
police car. People get on an underground train, a superimposed
eagle turns its head, we cut to the window of a Chinese restaurant
replete with hanging meat hooks, just before it is hosed down.
The eagle's head turns back. As the music gains momentum so
does the speed of the cutting. People run through the tunnels of
an underground station, in fragmented images a woman passen-
ger moves her bag closer, a tube train carriage rocks as the camera
peers through the adjoining window, a police car drives off, rub-
bish and the contents of a handbag are strewn on the street as
someone runs through it, two police officers walk the beat. The
camera zooms into the back of a car where a man sits smoking, an
advertising hoarding of a buxom woman promotes a sex shop,
two men in an alley tussle with one another, a man swills lager
from a can, a police van drives off with its lights flashing. The
camera pans out into an aerial view of the city at night and the
superimposed eagle flies off. Welcome to the world of *Crime
Monthly*.

This is a world where the streets are evidently not safe; every corner, every passer-by is potentially a menace. The city at night is mean, threatening, distorted. There was little, if any, concerted effort by *Crime Monthly* to reassure viewers that the world is fundamentally safe and the featured crimes exceptional. It is unclear in this credit sequence just 'who' the eagle is; the watchful eye of an ever-vigilant law and order, or the wild and unconfined spectre of criminality that reigns over the streets? There is no prompt here not to 'have nightmares' as Nick Ross would have it; the opening credits are absolutely the vision of an urban nightmare as every city-dweller's worst fears are brought to bear; the alleged influence such programming might bear on fear of crime can not be entirely easily dismissed.

The influence of film noir on *Crime Monthly*'s aesthetic was inescapably writ large across it, demonstrating again how the aesthetics of crime fiction, reconstruction and real life intermingle. Arguably the fictional film noir referent is, somewhat paradoxically, used here by a 'real crime' programme in order to evoke the *realism*, grittiness and authenticity of its vision of the world. But equally this style could be said to produce a kind of ambiguity about how 'real' this vision is, since one might also find a surreal or fantastic quality to this blurred, fast-paced montage of familiar urban images, a fluidity that once more demonstrates the generic permeability of media representations of crime. Noir referents also pervade the design of the set. The dim studio was lit in blue tones with red 'hot spots'. In contrast to *Crimewatch*'s presenters, who constantly stride across the studio resolutely, who stand, perch and sit at desks and by monitors throughout the programme, emphasising the show's sense of dynamism, breaking news and 'purposeful bustle' (Minogue, 1990: 23) the lone presenters of *Crime Monthly*, Paul Ross and later Penny Smith, overwhelmingly delivered the programme from behind a desk. While on the one hand this style could be said to reflect the conventions of news-reading more directly and is perhaps, then, an attempt to borrow from the gravitas of news customs, in this instance, and in comparison to *Crimewatch*, it has the effect of adding a certain static quality to the proceedings. It is hard to resist comparisons between the *Crime Monthly* set and the set of an archetypal Philip Marlowe office with the presenter rather emulating the image of the knowing detective behind his desk.[4] Smith sits in front of windows covered by closed venetian blinds. Behind her we can see a fan and a bottle (which in keeping with the theme would presumably be meant to hold 'liquor' of some kind) and the walls carry pictures of maps and wanted 'criminals'. Her desk is home to an anglepoise lamp, a large old fashioned black telephone and assorted ambiguous chrome objects. We can also make out a glass, a bottle of ink and a notebook. Curiously, and out of keeping with this classical noir *mise-en-scène*, above the window there is a bank of monitors. Ultimately then, the mix of technology with noir effects make this more *Blade Runner* (US, dir. Scott, 1982) than *The Big Sleep* (US, dir. Hawks, 1946); and like *Blade Runner*, it evokes a sense of post-modern disquiet.

The public service card wasn't played by *Crime Monthly*. In fact, appeals for information were just one element of its format. In this sense it was structurally more similar to ITV1's current real crime series, *Inside Crime* (2005–) than *Crimewatch*. *Inside Crime*, a more magazine-style show broadcast in half-hourly, pre-recorded midweek episodes and presented by well-known consumer affairs journalist John Stapleton, features only a couple of crime appeals, mixed in amid 'mini-documentaries' shadowing police involved in specific operations such as a campaign against speeding drivers (tx 25 August 2005). Similarly, in *Crime Monthly*, reconstructions of serious unsolved crimes and video/CCTV footage were featured along with 'Special Operations' – a mini-documentary where officers from a given division would be shadowed at work by a *Crime Monthly* reporter – and 'Casebook', a rather lengthy reconstruction of a serious criminal investigation where the perpetrator had been successfully brought to book. These two latter elements were clearly not about appeals for public assistance at all, but rather quite evidently about making 'real' police work into entertainment, with an informative slant.[5] *Crime Monthly*'s pitch, motives and aims, then, were arguably rather more frank and unambiguous than *Crimewatch*'s. Compare the opening passage from the *Crimewatch* book given at the start of Chapter 1, where they describe themselves as a 'serious information programme', with the words of *Crime Monthly*'s editor Jeff Pope; 'I'm not a great fan of the "public service" approach of *Crimewatch* ... I hope we are positively different. We go out later, so we can pitch the programme more directly at adults. We are certainly *out to entertain'* (cited in Minogue, 1990: 23, my italics).

Crime Monthly, then, was generally perceived as having a 'more downmarket image than *Crimewatch'* (Minogue, 1990: 23), arguably the result of channel identity as well as some genuine and significant stylistic differences between them. *Crime Monthly'*s reconstructions made undisguised, more prominent use of dramatic, eerie and sinister incidental music and would also more regularly feature effects such as slow motion, relying on techniques more readily associated with fiction genres. Furthermore, one could also detect a more apparent note of sensationalism in *Crime Monthly'*s use of CCTV footage. It relied more obviously on such material for appeals and would generally show these at much greater length than *Crimewatch.* Footage would be shown evidently above and beyond anything necessary to help make an identification; clearly the pleasure and purpose of showing such long sequences was not just to see if one could recognise the wrong-doer but to see the action, a theme I return to in Chapter 4. As Jo Scarratt and Tim Miller, who have both worked on both *Crime Monthly* and *Britain's Most Wanted,* pointed out in interview, *Crime Monthly* also included regular ironic digs at 'stupid thieves' and 'quirky funnies' caught on CCTV. This greater freedom and willingness to take a humorous look at such criminal behaviour, and take open pleasure in it, was again a feature which distinguished it from *Crimewatch.* This kind of approach to often disconcerting material has since continued to be wholeheartedly embraced by more recent real crime and reality TV clip-based formats such as *The World's Wildest Police Videos, Shocking Behaviour Caught on Tape* (Fox, 1998), *Dumber and Dumber* (Fox, 2003–), *Stupid Behaviour: Caught on Tape* (2003) and *Tarrant on CCTV* (2005) all of which absolutely pivot on the audience's horror, amazement and amusement at CCTV and video footage of 'stupid thieves', erratic drivers, comedic drunks and the like. Though Scarratt and Miller also emphasised, on a serious note, that *Crime Monthly* did get tangible results from its appeals, their sense of the fundamental difference between the programmes was best summarised by the word 'worthiness', as this exchange taken from my interview with them demonstrates:

JS: Crimewatch always sat there going 'Come on, phone up'.

TM: Oh it's very worthy.

JS: Crime Monthly was much more laddish.

TM: In your face.

DJ: He [Paul Ross] was a bit of a 'wide-boy'.

TM: Yeah, exactly. It was much less self-righteous and worthy. You see, *Crimewatch* has got this sort of BBC worthiness all over it.

JS: Yeah, 'do your duty'. (T. Miller, 2001)

In this account, then, Scarratt and Miller point partly to differences in channel identity; 'BBC worthiness' invokes longstanding stereotypes about the paternalism of public service broadcasting. Secondly, they highlight *Crimewatch*'s appeal to community, which I have argued is so characteristic of it, when they mimic its mode of address as the incantation to 'Do your duty'. By comparison, broadcast late on Friday nights, *Crime Monthly* was very much crime TV for the 'post-pub audience' (Campbell, 1993a: 2). Katie Thomson from *Crimewatch,* however, would very probably have thoroughly objected to such a characterisation of *Crimewatch*, since she evidently felt the programme does not patronise the audience, but rather goes to some lengths to work in a mature partnership with them. The following exchange, taken from our discussion of CCTV, underlines this:

> *KT:* I would never show gratuitous violence on CCTV but I'll always show as much of the sequence as possible. Because you know, we're not sort of Auntie Beeb, we're not trying to *protect* people, it is fair to let them see the action that you're seeing yourself.
>
> *DJ:* It's interesting that you say you don't see it as your job to protect the audience as that's been a traditional characterisation of the BBC.
>
> *KT:* That's why I don't like doing crime prevention. I don't want us being 'Oh, Auntie Beeb, you must lock your doors'. I want to give people a certain amount of credibility for their own intelligence. (Thomson, 2002)

In fact, the dramatic visual and aural effects noted above in *Crime Monthly*, such as soundtracks and speeded-up/down footage, were actually 'banned' in BBC news productions by guidelines announced in June 1994. Though *Crimewatch* claimed to have already put the recommendations into practice even before then, the new guidelines meant that 'incidental music, slow motion and other devices designed to give more impact will be banned from all BBC news and current affairs programmes' (Culf, 1994: 4). Other restrictions included: avoiding 'gruesome details of violent crimes'; including stories 'for significance and not on a disproportionate scale'; and, in crime reconstructions, 'no speculative detail' such as invented dialogue and no camera angles which place the viewer in the victim's point of view (Culf, 1994: 4). These guidelines were clearly introduced by the BBC as a measure to deflect criticisms about overblown news reporting and growing fear of crime. The then BBC social affairs editor Polly Toynbee was reported as having said 'crime stories [are] easy and cheap television with shock, grief and tears easy to come by. The BBC [has] to stand out against a trend inspired by newspapers and other broadcasters of being dragged down a sensationalist route' (Culf, 1994: 4).

The news reports above were referring specifically to the publication of the BBC's *Producers' Guidelines*. This is a handbook for production staff laying out the BBC's values and standards. As BBC director general Greg Dyke put it in his introductory statement in the fourth edition:

> [These Guidelines] detail the BBC's approach to the most difficult editorial issues and provide guidance which programme makers at all levels need to be aware of and to follow ... a succinct summary of the BBC's fundamental editorial values such as impartiality, accuracy, fairness, editorial independence and our commitment to appropriate standards of taste and decency. (BBC, n.d.: 2).

In practice though, the guidelines on 'Crime' and the techniques they refer to can be ambiguous and subjective and 'banned' elements are still far from absent in *Crimewatch*. More specifically, the section on 'Crime reconstruction in current affairs programming' includes the following guidelines:

> – we should not use incidental music or irrelevant sound effects.

- camera angles need careful consideration, and so do point-of-view shots.
- we should not frighten audiences with shots that make them feel they themselves are the victim, though sometimes it will be necessary to show a scene from the victim's viewpoint. The camera will usually appear as an observer of events rather than as a participant.
- we should not use slow-motion or other photographic post-production techniques which have no clear editorial purpose other than to dramatise. (BBC, n.d.: 151)

But if we look at the April 2000 edition of *Crimewatch*, for example, extended use of distorted camera movement and angles is drawn on in the reconstruction of a rape. This aesthetic is adopted to suggest the point of view of the victim, who provides a voice-over describing how she suspects she was drugged in a nightclub and then kidnapped. A series of images provide a warped and menacing vision of London's neon-lit Leicester Square, not a million miles removed from the opening credits of *Crime Monthly*. We open with the victim's point-of-view shot as she comes round. She lies on the step of a house she doesn't know, looking at the profile of trees above her which go in and out of focus against the night sky, as her voiceover explains 'I remember thinking "Oh my God, what am I doing lying on a doorstep?"' At some point in the preceding evening she was drugged, and taken to a nightclub. As she explains, 'Next thing we're in this place with flashing lights', we see her point of view of the club, a distorted montage of glaring neon and distorted superimposed faces fading in and out of shot. Clearly, very many special effects are drawn on here and they do achieve a striking dramatic effect. Their use would no doubt be defended on the grounds of their reconstructing the victim's subjectivity in a way that 'realistically' enacts her experience; but this is just one case that demonstrates how visual and aural effects are very much drawn on by *Crimewatch*. Furthermore, this case contradicts the declared intention not to put the viewer in the victim's point of view unless it is 'necessary', a term that is, of course, massively subjective. Rather disturbingly, the rape victim's point of view is re-enacted, not just in the establishing shots as she wakes up, but also when we see her attacker's hazy face looming in and out of shot as she is raped in a toilet and again when she lies on the street as he leers over her.[6] We see the victim's point of view again, for example, in the Sean Brown murder appeal in June 2005. In this instance, after the victim has been beaten and bundled inside the boot of a car, we are given a disturbing shot approximating his point of view of his attackers from within the boot of the car as they close it down on him; arguably not 'necessary', but most definitely dramatic.

In the May 2000 edition, the reconstruction of an armed robbery at a Barclays bank near Bolton, with its turbulent and vicariously subjective aesthetic, bears more resemblance to crime drama *NYPD Blue* (US, ABC, 1993–2005) than to *Police 5*. A fast-paced camera, compounded by jolting movement, extreme close-ups and jump-cuts captures the robbers rushing outside. As a policeman is shot we momentarily lose sound and move into slo-mo, showing the impact in fractured, fragmented movement. There are shots of the getaway car taking off which are speeded up, while slo-mo is used again at the end when the robbers abandon the car, piling out of it and striding towards the camera. It is a frenetic, distorted sequence that also builds drama through cross-cutting, and unfolds at times as if the camera had just been thrown into the midst of the action (rather than acting like an 'observer of events' as the guidelines recommend). The aesthetics used here, sometimes incorporating elements associated with the documentary aesthetic and sometimes action blockbuster, surely contradict the assertion that 'devices designed to give more impact' (Culf, 1994: 4) would be avoided in crime reconstructions at the BBC. Like *NYPD Blue*, this reconstruction borrows from or mimics the conventions of documentary to give a vivid, discombobulating sense of pace and movement that capturing events 'as they happen' can entail in such 'fly-on-the-wall' crime programmes as *Cops*. Once again this demonstrates the generic fluidity of real life and fictional representations of crime. As John Hartley notes in his discussion of the codes and conventions of TV news and their incorporation into other genres:

> In particular 'realism' somehow seems more naturally conveyed by a hand-held camera down there in the thick of the action and by the grainy appearance of news film shot in inconvenient lighting. Hence grainy shots and hand-held cameras have been

> exploited in aesthetic codes of filmmaking to express the gritty,
> unorganised subjective reality required. (1982)

The claim to avoid the use of music and sound effects is not
entirely borne out by the evidence, either, and again the guidelines on this area seem similarly open to interpretation. For
example, Operation Eagle, a serial rapist case in Bath featured on
Crimewatch in January 2000, makes much use of maps of the city
with dates of attacks superimposed over them. These images are
not silent, or accompanied only by voiceovers, but feature an
intermittent low, discordant *drone*, a low but unsettling non-
diegetic sound effect that is actually used quite regularly in the
programme. It works here to disconcert, emphasising the horrific
nature of the attacks and add drama to what might otherwise in
isolation be rather dull visuals. This unnerving effect is subtle but
deliberate. Other reconstructions incorporate diegetic music as a
marker of authenticity where the setting incorporates a home or
club or party, or to underline a historical setting by using period
music when appealing on an old case. In cases of the latter nature,
such as the murder of schoolboy Keith Lyon in Brighton in 1967,
the use of period up-tempo music adds not just historical authenticity but, incorporated into such tragic events, a sense of terrible
bitter-sweet nostalgia. Music is made all the more an emotional
marker of loss here in that Keith's father had been a big-band
leader. On other occasions music is again incorporated in other
deliberately emotionally affective ways; the dance music played
in the nightclub in the rape case above (April 2000) is muffled and
heavy on bass, for example, adding to our sense of the victim's
drugged and distorted perspective. One particularly striking use
of music (used in conjunction with a drone) comes in the February 2000 reconstruction of the murder of 14-year-old Marion
Crofts. Marion, we learn, was murdered on a country path next to
a river in Farnborough in 1981 on her way to band practice, where
she had played the clarinet. This particular detail from the case
enables the reconstruction to adopt an eerie refrain of classical
clarinet music as an intermittent motif throughout the reconstruction. While a montage of photos of Marion as a smiling
teenager unfolds, along with images of the news headlines that
announced her murder, the isolated strains of the clarinet

accompanying them undoubtedly add to their poignancy. To claim that music isn't used for impact in *Crimewatch*, then, would be disingenuous. It shows again just how subjective the producers' guidelines are in practice.

A decade after *Crime Monthly*'s arrival, *Britain's Most Wanted* was something of a hybrid of these two formats and the dramatic techniques described above are very much in evidence again. Where *Crime Monthly* was shot in a small office space, *Britain's Most Wanted* opened up the live studio space and mimicked *Crimewatch*'s design by having its bank of researchers and police officers (though fewer in number) staffing the phones in full view of the camera, staff who, as in *Crimewatch*, are constantly referred to for updates. The chiaroscuro lighting of its pre-recorded police interviews and the blue-toned studio lighting with red hot-spots recalled *Crime Monthly*'s noir referent. In fact, this colour scheme is common to all three programmes since it is also evident, in a more subtle fashion, in the *Crimewatch* studio; here the blue tones of the studio are broken up by red filters on the lights that fall on the partitions between the phones in the background. The urgent and recurrent use of thrilling music in *Britain's Most Wanted* recalled a James Bond film rather than a news bulletin, adding drama in much the same way as the menacing theme tune of *Crime Monthly* did. Both these theme tunes contrast with the upbeat punctuation, drum roll and positive refrain of the *Crimewatch* theme – an optimistic tenor underlined by its title, 'Rescue Helicopter' –connoting a confident march or military briskness of some kind. Again like *Crime Monthly*, *Britain's Most Wanted* is not only concerned with crime appeals. The summer 2000 series, for example, featured reporters shadowing a double murder investigation in Streatham, South London, filming at the crime scene itself and giving a virtually day-by-day account of the murder squad's progress, thereby combining an appeal function with police procedural or documentary interest.

Both *Crime Monthly* and *Britain's Most Wanted* were perhaps more reliant on visual gimmicks and hackneyed icons than *Crimewatch* allows itself to be and in this respect *Britain's Most Wanted*'s aesthetic debt to *America's Most Wanted* is particularly evident. The overall tone of *America's Most Wanted* is more overtly sensationalist than any of its UK counterparts. It consists far more predominantly of lengthy reconstructions, which often don't seek to name unidentified assailants but rather to locate known fugitives, and it even records the capture of some of them. Hence it builds in many arguably superfluous but intriguing 'character' back-stories for both criminals and victims, while featuring a virtually constant dramatic soundtrack – alongside urgent, insistent voiceovers, lots of spinning graphics and frantic montages – and it never shies away from slo-mo images of guns being brandished.

For example, the episode transmitted in the US on 23 November 2002 was 'Ladies Night', particularly given over to stories either looking for female fugitives or seeking justice for female victims, with presenter John Walsh's links filmed against the dramatic backdrop of Las Vegas. The programme's decision to film links on location, rather than in a studio brings with it the freedom to incorporate some visually arresting imagery that adds to its dramatic character; two weeks after 'Ladies Night' on 7 December 2002, for example, the setting was Miami, with its equally stunning night-time skyline. (Giving a rather more pragmatic explanation, the *America's Most Wanted* website notes that they avoid a studio since 'we try to work in the field as much as possible, right at the locations of crimes with law enforcement officials' (www.amw. com).) The first reconstruction on 'Ladies Night' seeks to locate an alleged murderer who also kidnapped his lapdancer girlfriend: cue lengthy scenes of their early relationship featuring her, scantily clad and gyrating in nightclubs. The second reconstruction wants to locate a robber, Heather Tallchief: cue lurid and heavily fetishistic scenes of her learning to shoot and blowing provocatively down the barrel of her gun. Walsh's cliché-ridden script reads like something from a bad Jean-Claude Van Damme movie at times, and incorporates an unfailingly disparaging and outraged commentary on the criminals sought, evidently designed to whip up the audience's fury too. 'We've got to get this guy off our streets, he's nothing but vermin!' he says of a rapist wanted in Miami (tx 7 December 2002); 'It's way past time to take down that dirtbag!' he comments on a wanted murderer (tx 14 December 2002).

America's Most Wanted's logo, with an eagle brandished across it, almost resembles some kind of superhero badge and the *Britain's Most Wanted* logo very much visually echoed this look;

featuring a huge letter 'M' in bold block lettering, it would spin round with a 'whooshing' noise to punctuate new sequences. This isn't to say that *Crimewatch* too doesn't make use of dramatic criminal iconography – the backdrops used on the sets throughout 2000, for example, consisted of huge panels reproducing enlarged fingerprints, though – given their scale – their appearance/aesthetic was rather abstract. As series producer Tim Miller saw it, *Britain's Most Wanted* enjoyed more freedom for innovation and development of the genre's visual aesthetics, a fact that again he links to channel identity:

> We tried to jazz it up from a kind of graphics perspective. *Crimewatch* has always been well behind *Most Wanted* on that. I mean I'm speculating ... but I think they've always felt a little bit uncomfortable about that kind of thing because they are the BBC. And this issue about making crime into entertainment, even though that's what they've been doing for the last 15 years, they've always had to pretend they're not doing it. (2001)

Like *Crime Monthly* before it, *Britain's Most Wanted* also allowed its CCTV footage to run rather longer than *Crimewatch* and longer than is strictly 'necessary' for identification purposes. The contrast with *Crimewatch*'s approach in this area can be seen in the way each handled the *same* crime in one instance. In March 2000 *Crimewatch* featured footage taken by a hidden camera showing a young man cajoling and confusing 85-year-old John Jones in his own home into handing over cash he supposedly owed him. The appeal was 30 seconds long, the film extract was 15 seconds long, the fraudster was identified as John Mitchell. In July 2000 *Britain's Most Wanted* picked up the case in an effort to find out where John Mitchell was; the extract taken from the same footage on this occasion was nearly *two minutes* long. Clearly, even though *Crimewatch* series producer Katie Thomson claimed above to want to show 'as much of [a] sequence as possible', they are more discerning or restrained in their use of CCTV footage than their ITV rivals.

Britain's Most Wanted would also show the same individual CCTV extracts more than once. For example, the first episode of the July–August 2000 series included footage of robberies shown in the previous series, since which arrests had been made, allowing the audience to see the crime in motion – though now without useful purpose – once again. Highlights from CCTV footage of violent robberies were frequently used as 'tasters' at the start of the programme to capture audience interest, then shown once or twice again in the actual appeal. The show also featured 'live at the scene' reports (the 'scene' being a police station where in fact no new developments are forthcoming).[7] It used a 'high-tech', reportage-style font next to its onscreen 'Wanted' photos, while in the black background behind the image, disembodied words reading 'Offence' and 'Most Wanted' and 'Illegal' floated by in green neon. When the 'Wanted' pictures appeared on screen a rotating image of a computer-generated, faceless head would be 'peeled' back to reveal the face of the criminal beneath, a graphic that appears in virtually identical fashion in *America's Most Wanted*. No such design excess is needed, or indeed tolerated, on *Crimewatch* in its photo appeals, where the image of the criminal and the authority of a police officer presenter's voiceover say all that needs to be said (though the images have been accompanied in more recent times by some up-tempo music). *Britain's Most Wanted* also made repeated entreaties to use email and it featured close-ups of the website and scenes of the producer Jo Scarratt working on a laptop computer. In fact, the repeated foregrounding of technology was arguably one of the most obvious ways in which the show sought to differentiate itself from *Crimewatch* at this time. Of course, the title of *Britain's Most Wanted* also clearly placed it as indebted to *America's Most Wanted*. This link could only have been detrimental to any hopes of respectability, given that the US show has consistently courted controversy for its voyeuristic and exploitative approach to real crimes (most infamously parodied by Oliver Stone in *Natural Born Killers* (US, 1994)), despite being the eighth longest running prime-time network show on US television (www.amw.com). But in interview, the producers were not particularly aware of or concerned by this link, and suggested that the criticisms of *America's Most Wanted* weren't widely disseminated in Britain; their primary motive was a 'dramatic title' that was more likely to get the programme commissioned.

Crimewatch's title sequence has been through a number of revamps during the programme's lifetime. In 2000, for example, it was a fast and fragmented montage. Thus in formal terms it bore some similarities to *Crime Monthly,* though it was far less menacing in content, for reasons I explain below, and its complete effect remains far more 'upbeat', given the brisk music that accompanies it. Like the studio colour-scheme noted above, the titles were expressively lit in noir-ish tones of blue, black and white with flashes of red. As it commences, disembodied single letters begin to spell out the C–R–I–M of *'Crimewatch'*, the effect being rather similar to a poison pen letter composed of newspaper cuttings. The series of fragmented images begins; there is a quick close-up of an eye, of a mouth speaking. The image is composed of multiple squares, rather like a split-screen effect. Then the full title *'Crimewatch'* flashes up but is only partly lit as a light strobes across, almost as if a search-light has just passed over it. An image of a CCTV camera follows, and it pans around as if to face us. A fleeting image of a policeman moves past and we cut to a flash of a newspaper headline. We return to the disembodied letters that continue to spell out *'Crimewatch'*. The 'T' is written in a flash of red; this colour is picked up a moment later when we have a flash of a colour image of a police car with a red stripe across its side. There is an image of written words on a page where one can just make out the word 'body', followed by an image of an armed policeman running forward. We return to the title with the 'searchlight' flashing across it, another image of an eye, and a series of three close-ups: one of a man with his hands surrendered up on his head; one of a man with a gun (whom one assumes to be another policeman by his calm manner and juxtaposition with the captured 'criminal' of the previous shot); and finally an extreme-close-up of eye, so close it pixellates.

To draw things to a close, we return to the letters spelling out *'Crimewatch'* till we finally get the whole word written out and fully lit on-screen. The effect of the whole sequence, as noted above, is a fragmented montage. Some of the shots are so quick they are virtually subliminal. And yet we can make a 'story' from these titles, we can find 'a kind of narrative image for its programme' from it, as Ellis suggested above (1994: 120). The 'synoptic' efect, firstly, is the omnipresence of *Crimewatch*; in amidst the flashes of criminal or law-enforcement iconography we repeatedly return to flashes of the title either being spelt out or partly lit. *Crimewatch*, then, is always there, literally in the midst of these activities. Unlike *Crime Monthly's* more indeterminate montage where criminal activity seems to be all pervasive and perhaps unchecked, in *Crimewatch's* title sequence from this period we have the reassurance, however brief, of seeing an apprehended 'criminal' in the image of a man with his hands up on his head. This image comes virtually at the end of the titles. It is this structure, then, that enables one to build a kind of abstract narrative from the images, whereby an unspecified crime is seen and reported on (the close-ups of an eye and mouth), investigated (the police), reported (the newspaper headlines) and solved (the surrendering 'criminal'). The initial close-up of an eye followed by a close-up of a mouth might be said to infer someone seeing something then telling someone. It is a synoptic image of a 'witness', then, the person who enables the chain of events leading to an arrest to happen and the appeal to whom lies at the very basis of the programme's remit. It is somewhat surprising, given their relative rarity in the UK and the programme's stated intention not to be sensational, that the titles feature images of armed police. But, nevertheless, the overall effect is an affirmative one of reassurance; we can watch these credits, which are dark in content at times, safe in the knowledge that though criminals are 'out there', they are monitored and apprehended.

More recently, the title sequence has been abridged. In November 2003, for example, only the *Crimewatch* logo being spelt out was used to introduce the show, while in June 2005 the programme used a curtailed 10-second sequence. This retains many of the same images and themes, however, and the same suggestion of a simple 'narrative' unfolding. The familiar format of a fast-paced, abstract montage played out across multiple screens is adopted; the letters C–R–I–M are spelt out, there is an image of eyes, of a mouth, the words '*Crimewatch UK*', a CCTV camera, a policeman and finally a 'Guilty' headline above a picture on the front page of a newspaper. In short, the brief titles still spell out the sequence and rightful order of crimefighting that the programmes exists to endorse and normalise: where witnesses (we the audience) speak out, cameras capture evidence, police arrest and criminals are convicted. Another key synoptic effect suggested by the title sequences described here is that of the ubiquity of surveillance and surveillance technology, present in the images of the eyes and the CCTV camera, concepts that are absolutely fundamental to the way the programme operates. In what follows in Chapters 3 and 4 I make a detailed analysis of how pleasure in looking, identification and surveillance all underlie the success of the programme and have been adopted more broadly as cornerstones of real crime TV.

In this chapter, then, we have seen how *Crimewatch* weathered the storm of the 1980s fear-of-crime controversy in the UK and can be differentiated from its less successful competitors on a number of bases: the abiding public faith won by the 'sincere' persona of Nick Ross as its longstanding presenter; its unique relationship with the police; and the enduring, though not unproblematic, resonance of the programme's claim to a public service function by virtue of its place on the BBC. We have seen too how even despite the BBC's claims to report real crime stories in a responsible and circumspect fashion, the interpretation of its own *Producers' Guidelines* is subjective in practice. Ultimately such guidelines do not safeguard against narrative and aesthetic practices that are arguably sensationalist in style and that seek to give the audience a thrilling, suspenseful, often visceral real crime viewing experience pronounced across the contemporary crime appeal format. In Chapter 4 I examine how this kind of viewing experience in real crime TV has been embellished by the growth and availability of CCTV footage. But first, in what follows in the next chapter I examine how this kind of vicarious entertainment has a history in the representation of criminality that long precedes television, as I look at the enduring fascination of still photography in the crime appeal format.

· NOTES ·

1 See Barker and Petley (1994) for more on this theme.
2 Broadcasting Standards Commission seminar at Cardiff University, 18 January 2001.
3 Figures obtained from the Broadcasting Standards Commission website at www.bsc.org.uk.

4 Philip Marlowe was the classic noir detective created by 'pulp fiction' writer Raymond Chandler and most famously brought to life on screen by Humphrey Bogart in *The Big Sleep* (US, dir. Hawks, 1946).

5 Indeed, in my own period as a press officer at New Scotland Yard I accompanied the crew filming these 'Special Operations' features on a number of occasions, capturing the Territorial Support Group in training and on duty around South and Central London. Careful editing in the subsequent feature emphasised the commitment, dynamism and danger of this work in a way that very much belied the long hours of uneventful driving, and indeed filming, that were necessary to produce a 10-minute spot. Police and film crew alike were concerned that nothing criminal would happen in their shifts resulting in a less than eventful impression of their job.

6 I discuss this reconstruction and issues surrounding the use of a victim's point-of-view shot in more detail in Chapter 4.

7 As in the case of the Sarah Payne murder inquiry, which was featured on the show tx 26 July 2000.

3 The Persistence of Vision
PHOTOGRAPHY, TEMPORALITY AND THE TV CRIME APPEAL

Over the next two chapters I examine how the emergence and success of *Crimewatch* and the wider real crime movement that followed it was enabled by, and very much continues to pivot on, the attractions and capabilities of certain photographic technologies. In particular, as I explore in Chapter 4, the expansion of CCTV as a new technology in the early 1980s could be said to have both contributed to and reflected some of the apparent preoccupations of the era. As we saw in Chapter 1, the introduction of *Crimewatch* and the growth of real crime programming was bound up in discourses and anxieties that were particularly prevalent at that time regarding the perceived breakdown of community, growing crime and shifts in the nature of policing. Another feature of these debates – and another crucial factor in the emergence of *Crimewatch* and growth of real crime TV – was the rise of CCTV, security cameras and video technology at this time. Hence, I go on to examine debates on whether real crime TV has actually contributed to the expansion and normalisation of a surveillance culture, enhancing its 'everydayness' and (arguably misleadingly) its reputation as a preventative measure in the fight against crime by embedding it in popular television (see, for example, Cavender and Bond-Maupin, 1993: 316; Derosia, 2002: 238; Couldry, 2003: 114).

But, in what follows I initially look at the importance to the crime appeal format of *still* photography, which remains a cornerstone of *Crimewatch* and its compatriots despite the growth of new technologies. This leads also to discussion of temporality in

the programme and specifically the conjunction of studio liveness with the 'that has been'-ness of photography (Barthes, 1993:
77). I contextualise the programme's use of images of criminals by
situating it within the historical association that has long existed
between photography and criminal apprehension, a relationship
particularly borne out by the relatively contemporaneous development in the mid-nineteenth century of photography and
increasingly more sophisticated police detection practices.
Images of *victims* in the programme fulfil a rather different set of
curiosities and cultural uses to those of the criminal. Here, I examine how photographs (and indeed video) of victims are often used
to underline victims' familial ties, be that through the familial
voiceovers and testimonies that accompany the records of their
image or through the inclusion of photographs that place the victim with family members and at family events. In this way I
suggest that *Crimewatch*'s use of visual evidence draws on two key
photographic traditions: the 'photo-story' and the 'family
album'. This is despite the fact that some commentators contend
that we have witnessed the 'death of photography', and are moving instead into a new, digital, era of 'post-photography' where
audiences are 'more reflexive, more "theoretical", more "knowing" in [their] relation to the world of images' (Robins, 1995: 29,
32). Arild Fetveit notes the seeming paradox that the rise of reality
TV has come about simultaneously with the rise of digital manipulation, something that 'has seriously challenged the credibility
of photographic discourses' (1999: 787). But, at the same time,
'the proliferation of reality TV could be understood as an euphoric
effort to reclaim what seems to be lost after digitilization ... the
powerful urge *for a sense of contact with the real* is inscribed in much
of the reality TV footage' (Fetveit, 1999: 798, my italics). Alongside the (often questionable) 'evidentiality' of reality TV, even in
the age of digitilisation this 'urge' for 'contact with the real' persists in our relationship with still photography. While the appeal
of a 'photo-story' underlines how, even in a multi- and new-
media era, still photography retains powerful narrative capabilities, the evoking of the 'family album' is evidence again of how
Crimewatch retains, adheres to and promotes conventional and
conservative ideological structures; in this instance, revering the

institution of the family and 'legitimising' victims through their placement within it.

Just as the development of photography has been entwined with that of criminal identification, then, so too has it been entwined with Western culture's representation and construction of the family. From the outset, for photographic technology to maximise its market potential it had to be consumed on a mass-scale as a leisure activity, shaped as a domestic product; thus 'cameras and films have been developed with the family in mind' (Holland, 1991: 4). In *Crimewatch*, these twin components of photography's evolution – that is, its foundations in criminal identification and domestic photography – are each returned to and evocatively drawn on.

The programme's insistence on placing victims within familial formations, as a means of emphasising their worth and the significance of their loss, perpetuates the notion that it is primarily through their roles within the conventional family unit that individuals can be positioned, identified and legitimised, thus endorsing the hegemonic institution of the family. Indeed, as I have argued elsewhere (Jermyn, 2001), the media coverage of the murder of *Crimewatch* presenter Jill Dando, including the *Crimewatch* reconstructions, recurrently marked her death as all the more moving, as particularly tragic, because it came on the eve of her marriage and thus her incorporation into the institution of the family. The ramification of this, as Michele Barrett and Mary McIntosh observe, is that, 'The overvaluation of the family devalues other lives' (cited in Holland, 1991: 7). Furthermore, as Cynthia Carter's work (1998a) has shown, this focusing on familial ties has particular ramifications for women victims in the media's representation of sex crimes, since their positioning as within or outside the conventional structures of the family is used as a means of indicating their relative 'blameworthiness'. My analysis of *Crimewatch*'s use of photography engages methodologically with Hartley's approach of 'forensic analysis'; photos – artefacts that he describes as 'mute witnesses' – become subjects 'coaxed into telling a story' (1992: 30). Thus, while I conceptualise the family album and the photo-story as core structures in *Crimewatch*'s use of photography, these are both more broadly underwritten by Hartley's conceptualisation of photos as 'talking pictures'. In his words, 'No picture is pure image; *all of them, still and moving, graphic and photographic, are "talking pictures"*, either literally, or in association with contextual speech, writing or discourse' (Harley, 1992: 28, my italics).

While, as I discuss in Chapter 4, CCTV and video may mark the zenith of the crime appeal's access to 'reality', the still photo is also enduringly very much evident as a staple and fundamental component of the appeal's structure. In fact, it can be argued that the history or development of photography takes place in tandem with that of modern policing and detection and that almost from their inception both were bound up in the functions of each other. Hamilton and Hargreaves suggest that 'The invention of photography was finally announced in 1839', while 'The use of photography to record the likeness of criminals can be dated back to at least 1841' (2001: 57, 101).[1] This suggests that virtually as soon as photographic technology became marketable, its potential as a tool of surveillance and social control was exploited. Indeed, Tagg draws out this link: 'At the very time of photography's technical development, the functions of the state were expanding and diversifying in forms that were both more visible and more rigorous' (1988: 61). I want to argue, then, that *Crimewatch* perpetuates the operation of a long association between photography and criminal apprehension, one arguably already in place by the mid-nineteenth century when photography (as CCTV would go on to do) became a means of making the criminal 'visible'.

· 'TALKING PICTURES' – CRIMINAL IDENTITY, HISTORY, PHOTOGRAPHY ·

The mid-nineteenth century was an era that was already preoccupied with attempting to develop systems of classification and order. Partly this is seen in the scientific endeavours of the age and their subsequent use of photography; the drive to produce taxonomies of race, social deviance and insanity where photography was used to identify distinguishing 'characteristics' and thus predictable and recognisable 'types' (Henning, 1997: 220–1). The massive expansion of British cities and population mobility in the 1830s had led to burgeoning fears of disease and crime. With the breakdown of traditional rural communities came an era where for the first time, en-masse, one might not know or recognise one's neighbours or the man passing one on the street. One could not be sure, then, of from whom or where disease and crime were emanating. Police forces expanded, as did the desire to develop more accurate and effective means of fixing the identities of suspects. The use of anthropometry at this time – an elaborate system of measuring parts of the human body – was a hugely laborious means of distinguishing one individual from another. With the arrival of photography, the development of the police 'mug-shot' was a massive technological advance that made it far more manageable to keep people under surveillance, fixing their image in a transportable and reproducible form. It is difficult not to draw parallels between the development and adoption of photography as a means of surveillance by police at a time of social malaise in the 1840s, with the harnessing of CCTV and video technology to criminal identification in the 1980s: a shift that was absolutely instrumental in and evidenced by the emergence of *Crimewatch* in 1984. This was a time when once again there was something of a moral panic ensuing around crime, policing and the breakdown of community in Britain, crystallised, as we have seen, in the contentious 'fear-of-crime' debates that preoccupied the media of the time (Gunter, 1987). There are similarly unresolved questions about determinism in both instances; to what extent did the development of the technology enable the expansion of surveillance – or did the desire for surveillance drive the development of the technology?

As the Victorian era went on, photography was used increasingly for criminal identification purposes, not just in terms of identifying the individual suspect, but in being able to identify criminal 'types'. The sciences of physiognomy and physical anthropology aimed to demonstrate that particular physical attributes indicated the propensity for criminality or other degeneracy and deviance such as mental illness. In Britain, Francis Galton pioneered composite photography – re-photographing portraits on the same plate by successive multiple exposures to create a composite image of a 'type' – in order to try to devise 'a new system of physiognomic record which would show the features common to three types of criminal; violent criminals, felons and sexual offenders' (Hamilton and Hargreaves, 2001: 96). The Victorians became fascinated with identifying criminals, not just in terms of locking up the deviant, but in the sense of being able to 'tell' what someone's physical attributes indicated about their moral fibre; in being able to distinguish 'them' from 'us'. It is this compulsion to look at criminals, to try to 'read' them, to try to spot the signs of their 'difference' that constitutes the fundamental allure of *Crimewatch*'s photo-montages of wanted criminals. Just as this fascination with 'seeing' fuelled the Victorian preoccupation with the classification and identification of criminals, it fuels the enduring popularity of *Crimewatch* and *America's Most Wanted*. As guides to physiognomy, detection and crime novels grew in popularity, the Victorian era apparently saw a change where many ordinary people fancied themselves as amateur detectives and pursued such knowledge as a way of alleviating uncertainty in an age marked by social and technological shifts; a zeitgeist that might equally be evoked to describe the *Crimewatch* viewer and the audience for real crime programming more broadly since the mid-1980s.

But what if we invert our dominant ways of reading mug-shot imagery? What if we try to understand its construction and circulation from the point of view of the criminal? Looking at Victorian mug-shot records, Ronald Thomas of Trinity College has commented that,

> Some cultures believe that having your photo taken takes your soul. Looking through some mug-shot files one can understand that belief. There is a kind of haunting quality to those photographs. A person has been trapped within the frame of the camera, imprinted for all time in a single gesture, with a single expression, defined by a technology which is entirely beyond one's control. (*History of Surveillance*, 2001)

Thomas goes on to explain the frightening circumstances in which such photos were taken; the suspect would have been arrested, restrained and faced with unfamiliar and imposing equipment. The photographer would have been an eerie figure hidden under a hood, the camera could have been mistaken for some kind of weapon; 'It look[ed] like a scene of execution' (*History of Surveillance,* 2001). Thomas is referring here to the period of the mid-nineteenth century, an age when photography was still a novelty, where the capabilities of its technology were still beyond the imagination. He demands that we reconfigure the way we understand historical mug-shot imagery here; not seeing it, as the preoccupations of the day would have had us do, as a fascinating insight into the physiognomy of the criminal, nor even only analysing it today as an instance of the Victorian fascination with classification, but instead to reflect on it from the perspective of the *photographed.* Specifically, Thomas asks us to consider how the context of its taking may have effected its apparent content, the demeanour and expression of the photographed. Criminal photography clearly, like any form of photography, was never capable of capturing an objective image; as a means of surveillance it would never be entirely 'scientific' in that human agency dictated its gaze. If, as Thomas calls for, we re-imagine the meaning of the criminal mug-shot by seeing it from the point of view of the photographed, an entirely new way of reading the image emerges, one that *Crimewatch* and popular culture's use of mug-shot imagery generally never attempts to imagine or open up. Indeed, John Tagg calls for a similar awareness of the significance of the context of the photo's making, and for caution about its relationship to the 'real', when he writes,

> We have to see that every photograph is the result of specific and, in every sense, significant distortions which render its relation to any prior reality deeply problematic and raise the question of the determining level of the material apparatus and of the social practices within which photography takes place. (1988: 2)

The way our culture has predominantly read photography of the criminal, our search for the signs of 'difference', the very fact of our fascination with such imagery arguably tells us more about ourselves than about the photographed.

· TELLING PHOTO-STORIES ·

Crimewatch, then, like all appeal programmes, makes significant use of surveillance 'evidence' of criminals in its appeals. But this material is combined with other visual traditions surrounding the image of the *victim*. This is another kind of visual 'evidence' that is crucial to the programme but which has been neglected in existing analyses of the programme, such as Schlesinger and Tumber's (1993). In fact, critical work on *Crimewatch* to date has consistently disregarded the extent to which the programme incorporates and is structured around visual records of the victims. This is a significant omission, since it is not just photos and videos of criminals that *Crimewatch* necessitates and pivots on, but the images of their dead victims. Susan Sontag has written, 'All photographs are *memento mori*. To take a photograph is to participate in another person's (or thing's) mortality, vulnerability, mutability. Precisely by slicing out this moment and freezing it, all photographs testify to time's relentless melt' (1979: 15). If all photographs are 'touched with pathos' (Sontag, 1979: 15) and the movement of time, if they all pre-figure death and the fragility of life, then the photograph of the murder victim is doubly charged with the emotive power of the medium. For Barthes also, photography is inextricably bound up with death, with 'that terrible thing which is there in every photograph: the return of the dead' (1993: 9). He too suggests that all photos are inscribed with the promise of the individual's inevitable death, and with photography's characteristic sensibility of 'what-has-been'. The photograph of an already dead person, then, is marked by 'the defeat of Time'; their photo speaks to the fact of both '*that* is dead and *that* is going to die' simultaneously (Barthes, 1993: 96). It is for all these affective reasons that photos of the murder victim compel and resonate so acutely in *Crimewatch*, and across culture more widely. Indeed, in one of the appeals I look at below, the murder of Emma Caldwell (tx June 2005), such was police faith in the affective power of her photo that it was projected 60 feet high on the side of a council tower block in Glasgow in order to encourage witnesses to come forward.

Real pictures of the victims, the stuff of family albums everywhere, pervade *Crimewatch*. In fact, one of the core aesthetic structures that recurs in *Crimewatch* is its use of a particular pattern of visual triangulation. In this structure, interviews with police officers or bereaved family members are commonly conducted so that a monitor featuring a close-up of the victim lies prominently behind them, between the presenter and the interviewee. Their picture thus forms a third point in the 'two-shot' which clearly seeks to underline the victim's resonance in this exchange. In comparison to the panopticist material of criminals, most often shown photographed unawares in public spaces by an impersonal surveillance camera or by a police photographer in the anonymous setting of a custody room, pictures of the victims are personal and private, taken from family functions, celebrations, in homes and on holidays. Sometimes photos of criminals are also drawn from such scenes; and this in a way makes them more fascinating, more shocking, than the mug-shot, since it places the 'deviant' in the realm of the ordinary. As we've seen, the primary or defensible function of the criminal photo is clear – they are shown to aid identification/apprehension. Beyond this, as the development of photography in the nineteenth century in tandem with the Victorian fascination with anthropological and physiognomical classification demonstrated, they also fulfil our inquisitive need to see what 'deviants' look like, as if they might look different from other 'ordinary' people. Photos of the victims fulfil similar desires while also satisfying an entirely different set of cultural needs.

These images seek to inscribe victims as ordinary individuals in the midst of extraordinary crimes, as members of families and communities. As with criminal photography, they provide evidence that satisfies our curiosity and almost rather primal need to see what these victims, these identifiably real people, were 'like' – that is, were they like 'us'? The familiar images drawn from family albums confirm that they were. Just as photography was virtually immediately harnessed to a surveillance function in the mid-nineteenth century, so too was it quickly drawn on to become the pre-eminent means of documenting the domestic. One could say, in fact, that the family album is another form of surveillance, 'tracking' one's history, origins, movement over years, through generations.

All the narrative forms at work in *Crimewatch*, from the updates on previous cases to the appeals and reconstructions, might be called 'photo-stories', since their accompanying voiceovers unfold around images of either the victim or criminal. Photos 'anchor' these stories and make them 'real'. The power of the photographic 'punctum', as Barthes named it, is consciously employed and manipulated by the crime appeal genre. He adopts the term *punctum* in *Camera Lucida* to express the capability of some photos to move the spectator, found in those photos where an element,

> Rises from the scene, shoots out of it like an arrow, and pierces me. A Latin word exists to designate this wound, this prick, this mark made by a pointed instrument: the word suits me all the better in that it also refers to the notion of punctuation, and because the photographs I am speaking of are in effect punctu-ated, sometimes even speckled with these sensitive points: precisely these wounds are so many *points* ... *punctum* is also: sting, speck, cut, little hole ... (Barthes, 1993: 26–7)

The programme's continual return to photographs of the victim in appeals and juxtaposition of images of life with stories of death seeks to employ the 'punctum' of every image. Even the recon-structions are 'framed' by pictures of the victim, providing an expressive way into their story and a poignant (quasi-)closure. In *Crimewatch* the victim's image is recurrently used to open the reconstruction – where typically the presenter introduces the case next to a monitor with the victim's picture on screen before we cut to a close-up of that picture – and to close the reconstruction, where we cut back to the studio after pausing for a moment on a still of the victim. The fascination with and implied stories that lie behind photos of victims make them a fundamental part of the way the programme is constructed. In just a handful of images the programme makers need to communicate enough about the vic-tim to make the viewer respond on some kind of emotional level, be that guilt, empathy, sympathy or outrage. Interestingly, although the photographic traditions at stake here may seem a million miles removed from one another – that is, criminal identification and the 'mug-shot' versus family photography – they are very much historically interlinked. While throughout the nineteenth century there was a burgeoning drive to employ the camera and photographic technology for the services of surveillance and classification, this occurred in parallel with a growing demand for domestic photography and social portraiture. The Victorian fascination, then, with social classification was evident in the way photography was harnessed to cataloguing *the family* as much as criminals and 'deviants'. In Hamilton and Hargreaves's words,

> There is a distinct sense in which nineteenth-century family albums can be seen as forms of the 'domestic museum', and the obsessive concern with their compilation is part of the nineteenth-century fascination with using photography to establish a complete, objective and comprehensive social inventory in a period obsessed with taxonomy and social order. (2001: 57)

Just as the composite photography technique pioneered by Francis Galton was used to identify the distinguishing characteristics of particular criminal types, so too was it used within families to produce an 'ideal family likeness' (Hamilton and Hargreaves, 2001: 97–8). Our fascination with photos, with using photography to be able to know, see, recognise, is as much borne out by the traditions of the family album as it is by criminal identification. The particularly compelling aspect of *Crimewatch*'s use of photography, then, is that it brings these two traditions together again.

· FAMILY ALBUMS – PICTURING THE VICTIM ·

In interview, I asked *Crimewatch* series producer Katie Thomson why victims' photos were drawn on so recurrently in the programme. In a reply worth quoting at length here she replied,

> We're always trying to say these are real lives we're talking about, this isn't an interesting reconstruction, this is a real person or family that's been destroyed. And home video helps a lot with that, because I think that has a real impact. It makes people

feel this person was moving and walking and talking and enjoying a birthday party six months ago and now they're dead. And
the same with their photos. I think if you had no image of the
real person you start thinking the whole thing isn't real. (Thomson, 2002)

This response points at a number of levels to the way in which
individual victims are typically constructed by the programme as
family members; she notes how it is not just 'a real person' who
has been 'destroyed' but by extension a family; she registers how
'home video' – i.e. film shot in *domestic* contexts – dramatically
underlines this context of loss; she specifically invokes 'a birthday
party', perhaps the quintessential familial celebration, to illustrate her point. Victims do not exist in isolation in *Crimewatch*,
but in numerous ways are very much grounded within family
units. They are constructed not as individuals in and of themselves but as spouses, children, siblings and parents.

This is seen, firstly, in the reconstructions that tell the story of
their murders but which also often provide 'back-story' by placing
them within familial contexts; secondly, in the interviews in
which bereaved relatives recall them; and finally, in the photos
and videos we see of them often taken from 'family albums'. In
some ways this entails the movement of 'private' media into the
public realm, also another marker of tabloid journalism values
(Annette Hill, 2005: 15), involving a kind of voyeurism where
moments from other people's lives, which were predominantly
captured for the eyes of their familiars and intimates, are laid bare
for all to see. Yet before critiquing *Crimewatch* for indulging this
voyeuristic tendency, one should also note the curious relation
the family album holds to notions of the private and public. On
the one hand family albums are consumed within relatively
restricted circles; yet they are very often made up of events and
spaces that are public, that involve a certain degree of 'performance' from the photographed; weddings, parties, holidays,
graduations.

What is more certain is that the privileging of the family seen in
Crimewatch's evocation of the family album is another way in
which it adheres to a largely conservative ideological framework.
Annette Kuhn argues that 'In the process of using – producing,

selecting, ordering, displaying – photographs, the family is actually in the process of making itself', largely adhering to culturally circumscribed conventions in the process (1995: 17). Though there may be room to 'read' these images in more oppositional ways – as Kuhn discovers in her subsequent deconstruction of her own family album – by drawing on the family album, *Crimewatch* contributes to the cycle she describes. It perpetuates the way that certain kinds of imagery constitute appropriate material for the family album and, by extension, that certain kinds of relationships, events and aspirations constitute the family itself. It is through their family ties that the victim in *Crimewatch* is primarily defined and, implicitly, valued, a disheartening sentiment for those who do not hold or preserve such ties.

For example, two of the most strikingly openly emotional interviews from 2000 were both with bereaved partners of young parents. In April, Bill Johnson is interviewed by Fiona Bruce about the death of his wife on Grand National day in Liverpool four years earlier. Walking towards a monitor featuring a large image of a young woman holding a tiny baby, Bruce explains that Pauline Johnson was knocked down by a hit-and-run driver five minutes from Aintree and that she later died from her injuries. This image (the 'third point' in the triangle) remains between/ behind Bruce and the bereaved husband throughout the interview. Bruce commences, 'Bill, thanks for coming in. You can see a picture of Pauline here behind us. Your son was just six months old when she was killed' – at which point we cut to a close-up of the monitor – 'How's he coping with it all?' Much of the interview that follows then primarily inscribes the dead woman as a wife and mother, cutting to focus on Bill as he explains how he has told their son that his mother is an angel who lives on a cloud in heaven. The tragedy of her loss is entirely grounded in her being the mother of a young child. There seems to be little space for any other angle or way of understanding who Pauline Johnson was and what she did in her life. Similarly in the case of Jay Abatan, murdered during an argument outside a Brighton nightclub, (May 2000) his partner Tania Haynes painfully describes how his death has left her to bring up two children alone. In the familiar triangulation structure again, the monitor between/behind her and Fiona Bruce carries a smiling picture of her and Jay together in happier times as she explains,

> It's been devastating for my family. We were a very happy family, we were a thriving family, life was good. The bottom line is Jay went out that night to celebrate a friend's birthday promising to take our two children for a bike ride the next day... [at this point we cut to a close-up of Tania speaking] ... and he never came home. And for me, as I would imagine for Jay, the greatest pain is the fact that my children have been deprived of his life, his care, his guidance throughout their years.

As the interview goes on, the monitor cuts from the still photo of the couple together to what appears to be a holiday video. This pictures Jay sitting outside in the sunshine at a table, i.e. moving and animated, just as his partner talks about coming to terms with his death. In short, ways of defining or remembering victims beyond the family are very largely tangential to *Crimewatch*. The testimonies of colleagues, friends, tutors or neighbours are all largely negligible and always secondary to the family. It is difficult to imagine a *Crimewatch* victim outside the parameters of the family; to not be in a family would be to not be a proper victim.

In *Family Snaps* (1991) Pat Holland argues that the enduring conventions of the family album operate as a means of disavowing the increasing fragmentation of the traditional family unit in contemporary Western culture. That *Crimewatch* places such evident stock by these kinds of images demonstrates its endorsement of this tradition. Paraphrasing work by Barrett and McIntosh again, Holland writes,

> Contemporary British society gives priority to an institution that is at best only partial and exists chiefly in what they call a 'familial' ideology which exerts pressure on public policy and social life. Family albums echo that ideology as childhood and leisure times are obsessively recorded. The camera is part of a lifestyle based on house, garden and car which moulds the aspirations of the suburban nations of the prosperous West. (1991: 5)

This description is potently borne out by the reconstruction of the murder of schoolboy Keith Lyon in the March 2000 programme, a reconstruction that is interesting also in that it is an old case (from 1967) being reopened due to advances in forensics. The foregrounding of time, memory, nostalgia, loss and historical authenticity that this entails make the absence/presence of the image even more acutely affective in this instance. Paraphernalia from the 1960s, such as clothes, buses and cars, all remind the viewer that this is a historical reconstruction, as do the extracts from TV news footage of the time, old newspaper headlines and the disjunction in the representation of Keith's family then and now.

The reconstruction is largely 'narrated' by Keith's younger brother, a sibling who is barely more than a toddler in the photos and cine-camera footage that are woven through the reconstruction, but a grown man in the 'now' of the appeal. Similarly too, the young mother to two small children in 1967 is transformed into an elderly woman interviewed in the present, while their father, the celebrity band leader Ken Lyon, is now absent and not accounted for at all. Keith's brother's voiceover opens with his observation that 'I don't remember anything before', but he recalls his father coming home unexpectedly on the night that Keith was found stabbed to death. As their mother explains how she was told that his body had been found, we cut to a black-and-white still of Keith as a little boy and zoom in as she notes, 'And that was the beginning of the rest of our lives'. His brother explains 'This was a time when my parents had everything they wanted really. A nice home, two children. They were very happy at the time'. Accompanying this description of the idealised family unit is a montage of cine footage that evocatively condenses a handful of choice moments and images. Their mother climbs out of a car smiling with Keith; the two children play in the sea with an inflatable; their dad cuddles the dog on the grass. These images do not foreground Keith so much as the whole family. They are images of the aspirational family, with as much currency now as they would have had in 1967; they condense the notions of domesticity, leisure and accomplishment with that of material abundance: cars, holidays, gardens, pets, even the fact of having had a cine-camera. The camera here has indeed been used as Holland describes, preserving 'familial ideology' in its 'obsessive recording' of childhood, leisure and affluence.

Similarly, in June 2005, the appeal regarding the murder of a young woman working as a prostitute in Glasgow opens not with facts about her death, but by taking us back in time. '1979. A little girl and her brother filmed by her family', Fiona Bruce sets the scene, as she introduces some old, silent home-movie footage, overlaid with melancholy piano music and the whirr of a camera. A little girl plays with a pram while her brother pushes it. 'The girl is nearly two. Her name is Emma Caldwell'. We cut to the image of a big block of flats, one wall lit up at night with the image of a woman's face; '25 years on she's remembered as a 60-foot projection on council flats in the Gorbals'. As we return to the home-movie footage, she is playing with her father and we can see now that a Christmas tree is visible in the background. Her mother's voice tells us, 'Oh she was a lovely child, full of fun. Just a magical child.' She loved horse-riding we are told, as we see a series of snapshots of her with ponies.

But this idyllic life was shattered; a family photo of Emma as a teenager with her sister is shown and we discover that Emma's sister died of cancer at a young age. As the appeal goes on it is predominantly taken up with the account of Emma's damaged family life and the events that led her to go off the rails. We learn that her boyfriend introduced her to heroin to cope with her grief, and later, she turned to prostitution in order to pay for drugs. Her eminently respectable parents are evidently horrified and devastated by this chain of events. Sitting in the family lounge with his wife, her father tells us 'We were rather naive about it ... and we weren't aware what Emma was doing to earn that money'. Pictures of her before and after she started to use drugs are shown side by side to document her decline. The final images of her life, in stark contrast to the home-movie of a little girl at play, are CCTV pictures of her by the lift at her hostel taken shortly before she went to work, and on the streets outside, on the night she was murdered. But this appeal is as much about family tragedy, an ordinary home randomly struck down by death and addiction, as it is about a murder. It is a story that viewers will be haunted by as they are struck by the precariousness and preciousness of this, and thus their own, family life: how did this little girl in the home video become the haggard picture projected on a wall, the dead prostitute in a field? These photos and home-movie images of

Emma's childhood and her origins in a respectable family life inscribed by aspirational values (riding lessons, loving siblings, happy Christmases, home technology), are clearly part of a narrative that constructs her as a legitimate victim whom viewers must seek justice for, not an anonymous prostitute.

Like a real family album (as Kuhn's *Family Secrets* (1995) has vividly testified), *Crimewatch*'s photo-stories are incomplete, fragmented, in that they can not depict every aspect of a life; they require the viewer to order and make sense of them, to fill in the gaps, which with 'our longing for narratives' (Holland, 1991: 1), we willingly do. The January 2000 edition of the show features a short appeal on the murder of Joe Bazra, a shopkeeper shot and killed in his corner shop in Glasgow, succinctly illustrating the drive to make sense of a 'photo-story' since there is no reconstruction, but rather a series of still images and video footage with a voiceover from presenter Fiona Bruce. It demonstrates how the programme must simultaneously personalise the victim, ground them within a family and appeal to a community ethos. As we see Bazra in a snapshot standing alone on the pavement outside his shop Bruce tells us, 'He was the sort of man we'd all like to have running our local corner shop. For pensioners who couldn't get out he'd deliver their groceries personally and he'd never let anyone go hungry if they couldn't pay the bill'. Both the ideal citizen (selfless, considerate, giving) and ideal community (supportive and close, frequenting local corner shops rather than depersonalised supermarkets) are evoked here. He stands with his arms by his sides, upright and looking straight ahead, almost standing to attention, framed in the doorway of his shop. The picture connotes his pride in having this shop, his own business; it had been a significant enough part of his identity for him to be photographed outside it. But there is also a terrible poignancy and irony in our knowing now as he could not have, that this shop, the source of his pride in this photo, would one day go on to become his murder scene.[2] Indeed the next shot brings us full circle, as we cut to news footage of the shop again, but this time masked off by police tape, adorned with flowers and with Joe absented.

As Bruce tells us that 'Everyone knew and liked Joe Bazra. They *really* feel his loss', the accompanying image is a formal portrait of him with two women, one of them dressed in a graduation gown, whom we assume, then, to be his wife and daughter. The graduation photo, that quintessential image of parental pride, individual industry and familial bonding is a staple of countless family albums and living-room walls, which many of the audience will have their own (virtually identical) versions of. Indeed, Jeremy Seabrook found in his ethnographic research into family albums that 'Although the photographs evoke personal memories, it is interesting to observe how many of these are shared by countless others. What seems to individuals a unique and, indeed, private destiny is in fact part of a wider social pattern' (1991: 178–9). The documenting of certain key images/events in our culture is so pervasive that such photographs cannot be thought of only as personal records, so much of their meaning and significance is ingrained and shared throughout that culture. The use of such images again ties the victim to familiar kinds of roles, spaces and values that the audience will, presumably, largely understand and share. It is interesting, then, that though the image of the graduation ceremony at this point shows Bazra as a family man, the voiceover refers to the bigger social context of his loss. We end finally with a picture of him smiling, in close-up. Joe Bazra has been shown both as an *individual*, whose loss has very personal ramifications for those close to him, and paradoxically as a kind of '*everyman*', whose murder was a random act, the like of which could impact on any of us. Joe Bazra's narrative, communicated in just a few words and images, is one of nostalgia but also family, hard work, community, drive and altruism – a narrative that is so pervasive and revered in our culture that it can be counted on to strike a familiar chord with viewers.

· (TELE-)VISIONS OF DOMESTICITY ·

This contextualisation of victims within families, then, is crucial for numerous reasons. Firstly, as series producer Katie Thomson indicated in interview above, it is a key component in how the programme perceives itself as being 'real'. Secondly, and related to this, it is of course crucial to the programme's audience address; our sympathy and empathy is very much sought by the inscription of bereaved families. As noted above, it is also particularly significant to the representation of women victims, since existing work on female victims of sexual crime has shown how their place as 'deserving' or 'undeserving' victims is recurrently constructed by the British press in terms of whether they adhere to conventional familial structures or not (C. Carter, 1998a). Finally, Thomson's attention to 'family' is significant in the way it bears out one of the key conceptualisations of TV within Television Studies, promoted by Corner (1999), Hartley (1992) and John Ellis among others, of TV as a 'profoundly domestic phenomenon' (Ellis, 1994: 113). In this conceptualisation the notion of 'the family' is absolutely central to television's operation, both in terms of who it perceives to be its predominant audience and in the preoccupations of its programming (Ellis, 1994: 113). It might well be inappropriate or misleading to describe *Crimewatch* as 'family viewing' (though it would be fascinating to ascertain the extent to which it is watched in this way; Annette Hill's reality TV audience research certainly suggests that 'police/crime programmes' were one of the most watched strands of popular factual television among both adults and children in 2000 (2005: 51)). But it is clear that it does approach the institution and sanctity of the family with the kind of reverence that Ellis describes as symptomatic of television broadly: '"The home" and "the family" are terms which have become tangled together in the commercial culture of the twentieth century. They both point to a powerful cultural construct, a set of deeply held assumptions about the nature of "normal" human existence' (1994: 113).

In the crime appeal genre the recurrent placing of victims within families affirms this 'normality'. We should note, of course, that just as Ellis decries the archaic inappropriateness surrounding television's privileging of the conventional nuclear family unit in the latter half of the twentieth century, television *has* had to diversify its conception of the audience since the era in which Ellis was originally writing, i.e. 1982. Nevertheless, the dominance of 'the ideological notion of the nuclear family' (Ellis, 1994: 115) that he speaks of prevails in the way crime appeals operate.

In an evocative image of television's intimate place in the home, Ellis describes how 'The TV set is another domestic object, often the place where family photos are put: the direction of the glance towards the personalities on the TV screen being supplemented by the presence of 'loved ones' immediately above' (1994: 113). Indeed Hartley's 'empirical but textual reading of the presentation of TV sets, and of the viewing environment, in the early days of Australian TV' (1992: 100) identifies exactly the same phenomenon. In his sample of pictures and stories from people recalling their use and 'dressing' of their televisions in the 1950s and 1960s, TV tops became 'shrines of family remembrance', adorned with photos of children, weddings and portraits (Hartley, 1992: 108). If Ellis's imagined viewer, and the descendants of Hartley's historical viewers, still style their home in this way, imagine the potency, then, of *Crimewatch*'s 'family albums' unfolding in this context. In this vision of the *Crimewatch* viewer watching at home, their own 'loved ones' in picture frames *above* the television are dramatically juxtaposed with the grief and loss now written into others' family pictures seen *within* the television frame on-screen. The domestic comfort or stability suggested by the idealised family album is rendered acutely unsettled, the family photos above- and on-screen contrasting in a conjunction where Barthes's notion of the photographic '*punctum*' reaches its zenith.

· REAL CRIME, REAL TIME – TELEVISUAL TEMPORALITY, LIVENESS AND *CRIMEWATCH* ·

At this juncture, it is worth noting that, despite the centrality of the photo, of the *frozen* moment, to *Crimewatch*, the programme simultaneously recurrently foregrounds its *liveness*. In *Camera Lucida*, Barthes speculates at one point that the fascination of photography must decline: 'And no doubt, the astonishment of "*that-has-been*" will also disappear. It has already disappeared: I am, I don't know why, one of its last witnesses' (1993: 94). The continuing success of *Crimewatch* with its attendant compulsion to integrate photographic evidence would seem to suggest otherwise. Intriguingly, though, alongside the fascination with still photography and its connotations of loss and the past, the programme's claim to liveness is another of its characteristic features and very much part of its identity; a large part of the 'buzz' of *Crimewatch* comes from its sense of ongoing, unfolding disclosure. Photography is a media that is very much characterised by the *past tense*; it shows a moment, passed, but captured. As indicated above, Barthes has famously commented, 'The name of photography's *noeme* will therefore be: "That-has-been"' (1993: 77). Because it is concerned with news stories as they unfold and narratives yet to find resolution, *Crimewatch*'s use of pre-recorded CCTV footage perhaps carries a particularly heightened and illusionary sense of immediacy. But, of course, CCTV footage is also ultimately about the past tense, and in appeals 'dead time' is often cut out to deliver only the edited highlights. By way of contrast, in Rath's words, 'Direct broadcasting occurs almost in real time' (1988: 32). What is particularly interesting about this conjunction, then, is that at the same time as the crime appeal format sells the spectacle of past-tense footage, a large part of its attraction and distinctive 'authentic' character lies in its foregrounding of its *liveness*. Indeed, Derosia argues that *America's Most Wanted*, too, situates itself as live, suggesting that it is 'prerecorded and assembled into a package of pseudo-liveness reminiscent of "live" television in the forties', where its 'direct, live address and the call for audience participation ... [act] as a barometer of authenticity' (2002: 243). In this section, then, I want to reflect briefly on the relationship and the exchange between *Crimewatch*'s interdependence on, and characteristic qualities of, studio liveness, on the one hand, and the past of its 'real' and reconstructed images on the other.

The whole notion of liveness has long been key to the way in which the distinctiveness of television has been conceptualised. As Rath notes, 'Direct broadcasting, live-TV in the living room, was the original television mode. The first twenty years of television programming – from 1935 until the late 1950s – were characterised by "immediate broadcast"' (1989: 32) (see also Couldry, 2003: 96). Discussion of the distinctive qualities of televisual liveness, then, constitutes an established debate within TV studies. For Jane Feuer, liveness becomes an organising *ideology* in television. She notes the peculiarly expressive quality of the term 'live' in the context of television:

> Television's self-referential discourse plays upon the connotative richness of the term 'live' confounding its simple or technical denotations with a wealth of allusiveness ... From an opposition between live and recorded broadcasts, we expand to an equation of 'the live' with 'the real'. Live television is not recorded; live television is alive; television is living, real, not dead. (Feuer, 1983: 14)

This conflation of 'the live' with 'the real' is, of course, particularly interesting in the context of *Crimewatch*'s overt staking of a claim to both. Nick Couldry argues that 'liveness' is 'a socially constructed term, tied not just to television's but the media's claim to present social "reality"' (2003: 96). For John Ellis, broadcast TV is distinctive for its 'framework of presence and immediacy' (1994: 135). Its various systems of address and representation collectively enhance a relationship between audience and TV screen that, according to Ellis, in opposition to that of the audience and cinema is characterised by familiarity and everydayness. This is inextricably linked to the fact that broadcast TV, as we have seen, 'is a profoundly domestic phenomenon', an object that is indelibly written into the spaces of our homes (Ellis, 1994: 113). Television's qualities of presence and familiarity are also particularly potent in its use of direct address. Ellis describes direct address as a 'powerful effect of TV' that encourages the viewer to feel part of an inclusive arena, something we saw in Chapter 1 as particularly true of the crime appeal format's evocation of community spirit. This effect is evident in the manner in which, 'Broadcast TV is forever buttonholing, addressing its viewers as though holding a conversation with them. Announcers and newsreaders speak directly from the screen, simulating the eye-contact of everyday conversation by looking directly out of the screen' (Ellis, 1994: 132–4). Significantly, Ellis suggests direct address also enhances television's sense of liveness. He notes that interviewers tend to conduct interviews as if speaking on behalf of the watching audience, drawing attention to the simultaneity of the media's temporal organisation, an approach highly visible in the way *Crimewatch*'s presenters constantly negotiate a line that falls somewhere between media professional and concerned citizen.

Ellis also suggests that TV's predominant use of segmentalisation as an organising principle and multi-camera editing enhances the sense that TV plays out in real time (1994: 143). With its organisation around discrete sections including reconstructions, updates on cases from that night and from previous broadcasts, 'CCTV corner', 'studio cases' and 'named faces' (the latter three designations being terms used by production staff, according to Belinda Phillips (2002)) *Crimewatch* very much fulfils the sense of television being ordered around the segmentalisation that Ellis speaks of. *Crimewatch*'s 'fragmentation' is evident too in the diversity of its parts. Its use of video material, replay of video 'highlights', different media (including photography, prerecorded video reconstructions, drawings, CCTV footage and live studio material) mean that it is, to adopt Feuer's terminology, a kind of 'collage' or 'mosaic' just like the 'live' Olympic games coverage and breakfast television she examines (1983). Ellis's attention to the use of the multiple camera set-up is interesting here too, in that there is still some dissent over the extent to which this practice, employed in much television output including *Crimewatch*, allows TV to reproduce the perceptual continuity found in theatre. As Philip Auslander notes, it has been argued that when the television director shifts between different cameras it produces an effect that might be compared to the roving eye of the theatre spectator; while the human eye will re-focus to take in different points of interest on the stage, the TV camera effectively does this for the television spectator, taking their eye to the point of interest (1999: 19).

However, Auslander objects to this comparison on the grounds that 'whereas in the theatre spectators direct their own vision, the television camera does not permit them to choose their own perspectives' (1999: 19). There are echoes here of André Bazin's contentious position that the long take in cinema represents the zenith of cinematic realism by allowing the spectator the freedom to decide where within the frame they will (shift) focus. This proposition negated the fact, of course, that the long take has already restricted the potential scope of the spectator's focus through its own choice of framing, angle and composition. At any rate, it is clear that *Crimewatch* makes great use of its multi-camera set-up as a means of foregrounding its liveness; there are constant cuts between the presenters seen at different points in the studio. They continually move around both within and between their piece-to-camera introductions to the programme's various items, striding to the phones one moment, standing next to a video monitor the next, as they work through photo appeals, videos, interviews, updates and displays of evidence. Space, dynamism and movement are suggested through their innumerable off-camera nods to one another or through the turn of their head as they 'pass over' to each other at the end of an item. The effect is very much a visual reminder of the programme's liveness that works in tandem with the continual verbal reminders that 'We're live as always' and 'Waiting for your call'. This style is a crucial component of the programme's identity, underlining the fact that updates and calls and investigative breakthroughs are unfolding in continuous real time. This, as we've seen, is very different to the sedate (even though live) style of *Crime Monthly* or the ultimately pre-recorded character of much of *America's Most Wanted,* but one that *Britain's Most Wanted* seems indebted to. If we agree that 'the multiple-camera set-up deploying three to five cameras simultaneously evolved specifically out of a desire to replicate the visual discourse of the spectator's experience of theatre' (Auslander, 1999: 20–1), we can agree too, then, that *Crimewatch*'s foregrounded deployment of a multi-camera set-up is an integral part of its foregrounded liveness; it adopts and utilises a form that can be traced back to television's early indebtedness to live theatre.

The televisual characteristics of intimacy and immediacy are particularly evident in *Crimewatch* in those moments where the presenters make a direct appeal to specific witnesses or callers who have been in touch but not volunteered their details. For example, in June 2000, in the case of the Mandy Power quadruple murder appeal (a case in which Power was murdered in her home along with her two daughters and mother), there is a direct address from Nick Ross to an unidentified woman seen in the area on the evening of the attacks: 'Please come forward yourself. Now, as you hear, you've got nothing to fear from coming forward.' The sense of intimacy is even more potent in the case of an update featured in the February 2000 programme. While Nick Ross is giving an update on the previous month's serial rapist case in Bath he makes a direct appeal to a woman who had phoned that night to say she too had been attacked, but who had rung off before giving her name. Ross tells her, and her alone, 'If you are watching, detectives have set up a freephone number pretty much just for you. Your anonymity is guaranteed by law, you'll be treated, I promise you, with the utmost sympathy'. The language here is striking in its use of the first- and second-person pronouns and in terms of the sincerity it proffers; a personal assurance is being made, a pledge held out by Ross and between him and this anonymous caller, though witnessed by millions.

Interestingly, given the prominence of 'community' we have seen in the programme's mode of address, Auslander argues against the proposition that liveness encourages a heightened sense of community. He suggests that a sense of community may arise from any situation where an audience shares common values and that mediatised performances are just as effective as live ones in operating as 'a focal point for the gathering of a social group':

> My point is simply that community is not a function of liveness. The sense of community arises from being part of an audience and the quality of the experience of community derives from the specific audience situation, not from the spectacle for which that audience has gathered. (Auslander, 1999: 56)

However, in opposition to Auslander, Rath has argued that live broadcasts *do* operate in a manner that enhances the audience's perception of belonging to a television community:

> The specific uniqueness implied here is signified by the collective, simultaneous perception of an event charged with symbolic value. In this sense, we can say that something like a 'live aura' exists. It inscribes its audiences into the social order of what can be called the 'television community'. (Rath, 1989: 88)

He also notes how live TV can offer the audience the opportunity to participate in a number of ways, including calling dedicated phone lines, a function absolutely integral to *Crimewatch*, of course. These 'real-time interventions' operate not just as a mode of participation but also as 'a kind of guarantee of simultaneity' (Rath, 1989: 88). Liveness, then, is another characteristic bound up in the 'realism' of *Crimewatch*. Its sense of authenticity is enhanced not just through the potent significance given to real images of criminals and victims and the presence of real police presenters, but through its real time. We are continually reminded that live tonight, before us, a breakthrough may unfold. The Marion Crofts murder inquiry, for example, has remained unsolved for 20 years; but, potentially, 'tonight, at long last, prompted by what you're about to see, someone might just open up their heart and call in with their suspicions' (February 2000). As Rath puts it, 'Like dramatic incidents on the street or in the family, "live" television is endowed with the special notion of an encounter with the "real". Its particular attraction lies in the promise of the unforseeable' (1989: 85).

One notion that Rath and Auslander share, however, is scepticism about how 'live' live broadcasts really are. For Auslander, in an increasingly mediatised world, 'Live performance now often incorporates mediatization such that the live event itself is a product of media technologies' (1999: 24). For him it is a 'reductive binary opposition' to conceptualise the live and the mediatized as polar; this seems particularly pertinent to *Crimewatch*, given that actually this 'live' broadcast depends to a very large extent on previously recorded material in the reconstructions. However, in interview assistant producer Belinda Phillips suggested that, apart from re-opened old cases, even *Crimewatch's reconstructions* carry a sense of topicality, if not immediacy, that enhances the programme's sense of liveness. They deliberately seek to include cases from the last few days, although these are inherently more risky material because of the greater possibility of breakthroughs in the interim between filming and broadcast, 'to try and keep it feeling as if *this in on the go*' (Phillips, 2002, my emphasis). Through this, through maximising its use of television's characteristic mode of direct address, through the prominent clock featured on the presenters' main desk, through the constant reiteration that a breakthrough call could happen at any time – even as we watch – *Crimewatch* very capably orchestrates a 'live aura' even despite its reliance on past-tense media.

In this chapter, then, we have seen how the crime appeal genre pivots on the structures, meanings and pleasures afforded by visual records of victims and criminals. The ideological and social frameworks contained within these are largely conventional and familiar: the fascination with looking for the signs of 'difference' in the deviant criminal; the spectacle of criminal identification and apprehension; the containment and definition of the individual within the structures of the family; the pre-eminence and privileging of membership of the traditional family as a legitimate and revered norm. While we should not presume that viewers do not engage in multiple and/or oppositional ways with the programme, nevertheless in promoting these themes *Crimewatch* works to marginalise other ways of thinking about criminals and victims that would prove problematic to its representations, that would risk rupturing its generally uncomplicated vision. Indeed, Gareth Palmer, writing about *Crimewatch* along with *Crimebeat* and *Crime Squad*, has argued that these programmes evidence a new focus on 'the victim' in crime programming. He argues that, as such, they are part of larger trend in this period to evade a more rigorous contextualisation of crime, a deflective strategy that seeks to 'shift the public's attention away from the inexplicable nature of the offender, and his or her social origins, and towards the responsibilities of the community' (Palmer, 2003: 70). In a similar vein, the troubling fact of the increasing fragmentation of the traditional family unit is absented in this discourse, as victims are enduringly 'pigeon-holed' into easy and identifiable familial roles, a kind of shorthand for legitimising both them (as innocent and undeserving victims) and the hegemonic institution of the family itself. Through its refusal to engage with the experiences, contexts or perspectives of 'the criminal' in these 'snapshots' of crime, the programme steadfastly evades opening up diverse or oppositional discourses around criminality, falling back instead on the age-old fascination of the singular, defining image of the criminal deviant. As I will now examine, with the advent of CCTV and the expansion of home video technologies in the 1980s came new ways and opportunities to pursue these old fascinations.

· NOTES ·

1 There is some difference of opinion here with Tagg, however, who notes, 'In Britain, local police forces had been using photography since the 1860s' (1988: 7).
2 This is a particular potency drawn on again in the widely published picture of the murdered *Crimewatch UK* presenter Jill Dando, circulated just after her murder, where she is captured standing on her doorstep in a photo taken a few weeks before she was to be shot there. For a detailed discussion of the media's representation of Dando's murder see Jermyn, 2001.

4 Someone to Watch Over Me

CCTV AND SURVEILLANCE IN REAL CRIME TV

In the 1980s, innovations in video technology crucially provided novel 'actuality' material for emergent real crime TV formats, tapping into, and arguably exacerbating, the preoccupations of an era marked by the rapid growth of CCTV camera systems. In what follows I look at the circumstances leading to this growth and at debates examining whether real crime TV has actually contributed to the normalisation of a surveillance culture. Diffusing the disquieting nature of the practice of surveillance by rendering CCTV as 'entertainment' on the one hand (e.g. *Tarrant on CCTV* (ITV, 2005)), and as an indispensable tool in criminal identification and apprehension on the other (e.g. *Crimewatch*), the end result of the myriad reality TV movements drawing on CCTV footage arguably has been to foster a popular acceptance of surveillance as a familiar and inevitable condition of contemporary life. However, TV is not merely a 'culture industry', but a business driven by economics. CCTV also crucially provided *affordable* material to be capitalised on in new programmes during a period of de-regulation in an expanding and increasingly commercial television industry. The growth of what Annette Hill calls 'reality clipshow formats' (2005: 8) since the early 1990s as an offshoot of crime and emergency services programmes (her examples range from *When Animals Attack* to *World's Worst Drivers Caught on Tape 2*) evidences just how profitable the acquisition of this kind of unscripted footage has become to some programme makers who build entire series round such material.

Programmes such as *Police Camera Action!* and *World's Wildest Police Videos* consist almost wholly of montages of police footage of car chases and arrests, while in a further development *America's*

Dumbest Criminals presents 're-enactments' of crimes, mixed in with genuine CCTV/police footage, which fake the appearance of CCTV and surveillance material while the presenter relates what happened. Other real crime TV programmes, such as *Traffic Cops* and *Shops, Robbers and Videotapes* rely heavily on CCTV footage – in the latter instance consisting of material obtained from shops and malls capturing shoplifters on tape – but mix this in with police/security interviews and more conventional documentary-style footage obtained while 'shadowing' them at work. In the latter part of this chapter I examine the implications of the growth in real crime TV 'clipshow' programmes such as *Police Camera Action!* and *World's Wildest Police Videos*, asking whether we might understand these programmes to be less ideologically conservative in their function than their crime appeal predecessors, since their spectacle is enjoyed with a less overtly moral purpose/ project.

All of these formats, then, make for budget television and, as Hill has observed, the broader rise of reality TV was marked by the economic imperatives of the period;

> The rise of reality TV came at a time when networks were looking for a quick fix solution to economic problems within the cultural industries. Increased costs in the production of drama, sitcom and comedy ensured unscripted, popular factual programming became a viable economic option during the 1990s. The deregulation and marketisation of media industries, especially in America and Western Europe, also contributed to the rise of reality TV, as it performed well in a competitive, multi-channel environment. (Annette Hill, 2005: 39; see also Dovey, 2000: 83–4)

Clearly, though, there is more than economics, and the peculiarities of the era's socio-political climate, at stake in the growth of the real crime genre. I argue here that these programmes respond to and perpetuate our culture's *perennial* fascination with seeing criminals and victims, indulging a longstanding taste for the spectacle of criminal apprehension and punishment – pleasures that are anything but novel and which very much precede 'new technologies'. For example, writing in *The Listener* in 1989, Bob Woffinden had this to say about the work of *Crimewatch*:

Crimewatch has an enhanced entertainment value; quite simply, it's better because it's real. A kind of blurring of distinctions thus occurs. One wonders to what extent *Crimewatch* appeals to its audience on a voyeuristic or salacious level. It's hardly a public hanging, but is it a kind of contemporary equivalent, catering to similarly unworthy sensibilities? It is certainly akin to a hanging and to the tabloids' presentation of crime in that it requires the perpetrators of crime to be beyond the reach of common humanity. (1989: 10)

Woffinden's condemnatory appraisal of the programme is intriguing for a number of reasons. First, it equates its proximity to the 'real' as enhancing its entertainment credentials rather than any claim to be 'informative'. Second, it exhibits a now familiar nervousness about the programme's perceived 'blurring' of boundaries. Finally, it invokes comparisons, not merely to the tabloid press – discourses that the programme is indeed indebted to, as we have seen – but to *'public hangings'*; that most appalling, but most spectacular, enactment and celebration of the apprehension and punishment of criminals (see Garland, 1991, and Gatrell, 1994). His casual reference to this historical vision of the spectacle of crime perfectly captures the kind of cultural fascination at stake here, which crime appeals perpetuate, surrounding our pleasure in publicly 'naming and shaming' criminals. More broadly, by examining the allure of *Crimewatch* and its compatriots we can identify how an enduring attraction at their core is the *spectacle of actuality*, a pleasure that both precedes the television crime appeal and which other subsequent real crime and reality TV formats have explored and exploited with a renewed enthusiasm.

CCTV technology has come to enjoy a distinctive relationship with actuality and 'the real'. As Jon Dovey notes,

The low-grade video image has become *the* privileged form of TV 'truth telling', signifying authenticity and an indexical reproduction of the real world; indexical in the sense of presuming a direct and transparent correspondence between what is in front of the camera lens and its taped representation. (2000: 55)

Equally, the spectacle and promise of CCTV material is one of the fundamental allures of crime appeal programming for its audience. While the genre's adoption of CCTV in the mid-1980s, as indicated above, may have been a celebration of the spectacular properties of '*new*' technologies, the primary appeal of CCTV is very much historically evident in longstanding cultural discourses celebrating 'actuality'. Furthermore, in seeking to understand the compelling nature of CCTV (and video footage more broadly), we must recognise how one of its most potent features lies in the manner in which the medium pivots on an affective temporal conjunction. In CCTV a heightened illusion of *immediacy* converges with the *past-tense* status it holds in common with all visual records. This potency is one of its most fascinating elements, but it also highlights how much more than mere criminal apprehension and identification is at stake in the crime appeal's embracing of such footage, since it is arguably at its most affective in the genre's recollection and representation of *victims*; the spectacle of actuality extends equally to both groups.

The act of representing the victim constitutes a process whereby everyday and 'ordinary' people are transformed by circumstance and media attention into the 'extraordinary', a discourse characteristic of many reality TV formats, in fact. Hence it is not surprising that, in a media reception similarly marked by disquiet and unease, striking parallels to the debates about crime appeal programming seen in the 1980s/early 1990s emerge again in the discourses about reality TV that have predominated in the late 1990s and early 2000s. For example, in 2002, *Guardian* TV critic Gareth McLean observed in his 'Comment' column that 'the attraction of the genre is hard to explain ... call it rubbernecking or empathising but everyone loves watching a tragedy being played out don't they?' This account seems a pertinent and concise summary of our double-edged fascination with *Crimewatch*'s stories of loss and violence – but in fact it was written to accompany an article about ITV's *Popstars: The Rivals* (McLean, 2002: 7). Debates about 'quality', public service, cynical and irresponsible programme makers, commercial pressures and generic 'blurring' have all similarly been drawn on in the opposition that has met the emergence of 'reality TV' since the late 1990s. The parallels are more than coincidental: with its popularisation of reconstructions, its claiming of 'real' stories and testimony from real witnesses, its privileged relationship with 'actuality' via the incorporation of authentic CCTV/video/photography, its appeal to a mass audience to take a participatory role in a contentious television format and its evoking of that audience as an '(inter)active' one who through their phone call can play a role in actually shaping the programme as it unfolds – all of which come together in a kind of hazy territory where social project and entertainment meet – *Crimewatch*'s status as a major forerunner to the emergence of numerous strands of the current reality TV movement seems increasingly apparent.

· REINVENTING SURVEILLANCE CULTURE ·

Crimewatch was not alone in identifying the televisual potential of new video technologies in this period, as evidenced by the subsequent appearance of a whole array of reality TV programming that pivoted on the use of video and CCTV material (much of it not specifically concerned with crime appeals), including *999* (BBC, 1992–), *Police Camera Action!* (ITV, 1994–), *Crimebeat* (BBC, 1995–9), *EyeSpy* (LWT, 1995–9), *Video Diaries* (BBC, 1990–9) and *Video Nation* (BBC, 1994–2000). Indeed, Dovey has described this televisual development, rather apocalyptically, as constituting the medium's 'sudden viral contamination by camcorder and surveillance footage' (2000: 57). The explosion of reality TV generally since the 1990s, then, has taken up the initiative originally pursued by the crime appeal genre to make CCTV footage a regular component of contemporary television programming. Within this it has also repositioned (or arguably consolidated[1]) its status as an *entertainment* form, where its use is increasingly less controversial and more an everyday part of the televisual landscape.

For example, *Tarrant on CCTV* consists of a variety of CCTV clips presented by the popular TV quiz host Chris Tarrant, obtained from diverse sources, from US police to offices and supermarkets in the UK, and selected for their 'comedic' value. A student in a locker room is caught 'inappropriately' using someone else's towel; a man sniffs his co-worker's shoes when she leaves the office (tx ITV, 1 August 2005); but at no point does the programme question the ethics of having CCTV installed in these spaces, presumably without the knowledge or consent of the people using them. These moral issues are diminished by the positioning of the clips as 'entertainment', as well as by reminders that in these instances the cameras really do, in Tarrant's words, 'catch people off-guard'. Hence, Palmer has suggested that, at a broader social level, programmes such as *Crimewatch*, *Crimebeat* and *Crime Squad* share an 'advocacy of increased surveillance' (2003: 87). Furthermore, Biressi and Nunn note that one of the repercussions of the 'scopic colonisation of public space' and its subsequent adoption by reality TV formats is that, 'These depictions in turn help form the imaginary relationship between policing and the public'. They suggest that the police have become increasingly allied with televisual technology in factual programming, reinforcing the illusion 'that the police, like television itself, seem to be ubiquitous, always present whether visible or not' (Biressi and Nunn, 2005: 126).

It was at the point of *Crimewatch*'s debut, then, from the mid-1980s, that video and surveillance technology became increasingly accessible and affordable on a wide scale, moving beyond banks and building societies into small shops and businesses and eventually, of course, to high streets, car parks and public places of every nature across the country. The first public CCTV scheme in Britain was launched in the seaside resort of Bournemouth in August 1985; just a decade later Britain had 'more public space CCTV systems than any other advanced capitalist nation' (Fyfe and Bannister, 1998: 257) and by 2000 the CCTV industry was worth more than £300m in Britain every year (*History of Surveillance*, 2001). By the early 1990s, then, the growth of this technology was such that it impacted on national everyday life – in the words of *Guardian* crime correspondent Duncan Campbell,

> To those of you who have always wanted to be in films – congratulations, you've made it. If, in the last 24 hours, you have gone shopping, travelled to work, visited a post office, taken a train, watched a football match, put petrol in your car, visited the off-licence, or walked through a city centre, you will have played at least a small part in the one section of Britain's film industry that is experiencing astonishing growth: video surveillance. (1993a: 2)

This shift didn't occur entirely without anxiety or opposition; campaign groups such as Liberty drew attention to issues of legislation, statutory control and personal privacy. Groups like the 'Surveillance Camera Players' who stage protests around CCTV sites have emerged in the US while in the UK, Ian Toon has described how disenfranchised young people in Tamworth town centre have formed strategies of resistance to surveillance cameras, identifying and exploiting camera 'blindspots' and splitting into small groups to fragment the regulatory gaze (2000: 155). But on the whole it appeared that the opportunities the technology offered for crime reduction and detection outweighed the concerns. Implicit in this was a sense that only those who were somehow complicit in crime would resent the introduction of CCTV; as a culture 'by and large we have bought the idea that "only the guilty have anything to fear"' from its use (Dovey, 2000: 66).

However, the arguments in favour of CCTV are by no means incontrovertible. Fyfe and Bannister suggest that 'there is little consistent research evidence' to sustain claims that CCTV deters and reduces crime and, indeed, that the presence of cameras might even be displacing crime to other areas out of camera range (1998: 257; see also Lydall, 2003). Simon Davies, the director of Privacy International, has similarly maintained that CCTV merely relocates rather than eradicates crime. But, intriguingly, he further suggests that the misconception that CCTV is a deterrent against crime is one that has actually been popularised by the media and crime appeal programmes *themselves*, through their recurrent broadcasting of CCTV crime footage in crime appeals. He points to the absurdity of this:

> The reason people believe [CCTV] *affects* crime is because they keep seeing the images on TV – and bizarrely people are watching images of crime being commissioned and yet *strengthening* their belief that the technology can stop crime. It's a non-sequitur. CCTV does not cut down crime. (*History of Surveillance*, 2001)

Furthermore, rather than gratifying the public with a sense of enhanced security, it may be the case that for some people surveillance systems can actually have the opposite, detrimental effect, heightening paranoia, suspicion and fear of crime by 'signpost-ing' the possibility of crime.

Fyfe and Bannister (1998) suggest that the growth of CCTV in inner city areas and high streets must be seen within the context of a broader economic, socio-cultural and political agenda at that time, in this instance promoting the privatisation and commodi-fication of public space. For example, Toon contextualises his study of CCTV surveillance and young people in Tamworth city centre with an account of how British town centres underwent a period of economic decline during the 1980s. A growing sense of alienation from these spaces was noted as a key component in ris-ing fear of crime. The most visible response to this since the 1990s has been to try to revive the town centre's economic role. In the drive for urban renewal, 'powerful commercial and civic interests have embraced shopping and leisure as a key economic strategy' (Toon, 2000: 148). But these are not inclusive spaces; with their low spending power, Toon found that these youths were consist-ently 'moved on' by police, compounding and perpetuating cultural assumptions about young people as 'troublemakers' to the extent that they have become a kind of underclass (2000: 149). In this way, many of the key preoccupations of the 1980s zeitgeist in Britain – fear of crime, law and order politics, the demise of 'community', a bid for economic renewal – come together to intersect in the heavily surveilled space of the regener-ated town centre. Hence *consumerism*, rather than crime alone, appears to be a significant impetus behind the popularisation of CCTV, a notion very much borne out internationally, and in the US particularly, by the concurrent and intertwined growth of CCTV and shopping malls.

Though these technological developments are now well estab-lished, at the time of their introduction they heralded in a 'new' kind of crime discourse centred around contemporary forms of surveillance. They entailed a movement that perfectly fulfilled the needs (or, to look at it another way, *enabled* the development) of *Crimewatch* and its like. Not only do *Crimewatch* and *Britain's Most Wanted* draw regularly on CCTV in their appeals, both use 'surveillance footage' as a visual referent in their title sequences, concurring with Helen Wheatley's observation that CCTV foot-age has become 'the trademark of real crime programming' (2001:

46). *Britain's Most Wanted*'s opening montage, for example, featured genuine footage of arrests and raids as well as more abstract images of technological and surveillance devices including fingerprints, thermal imaging, a cross-hair shifting focus and a double-helix symbol signifying DNA science. All of this is accompanied by the *Britain's Most Wanted* dramatic signature tune, adding up to a fast action-packed sequence that foregrounds detection, technology, surveillance and science in the manner of a thriller. Similarly, one of the show's recurrent icons was the use of a superimposed camera 'cross-hair' (as also seen in rifle viewfinders, in fact) to 'frame' the CCTV footage shown and move into it when focusing into a close-up. Tim Miller, the series producer of *Britain's Most Wanted*, suggested that the aesthetic quality of the zoom in his programme's use of surveillance footage was essential to the programme's style, adding to the dramatic weight given to the CCTV footage. In his words, 'It's quite exciting. There's something about zooming in on something that is exciting in a way that just seeing it happen wouldn't be. It gives it added emphasis. And also when you zoom into something the image becomes bigger' (T. Miller, 2001). Discussing these motifs further, his comments point to the real crime and crime appeal formats' simultaneous fascination with, and contribution to, contemporary surveillance culture:

> I think the idea of that sort of 'surveillance camera' was basically like you're being the criminal, you're being watched out there. I don't want to get too grand about it, but it's like a kind of metaphor for our viewers' contribution, isn't it? Like everyone out there can see it, you can see it, you're going to be caught, you're being watched, you've been warned type of thing. (T. Miller, 2001)

What's interesting about his description here is its apparent blurring of criminal and public under the camera's watchful eye. This surveillance technology isn't just watching the criminals – it's watching *all* of us. So while his description starts off imagining the surveillance imagery as vicariously placing us in the criminal's position ('like you're being the criminal') what it also demonstrates is that not only 'everyone out there can see it', but equally, 'everyone out there' is 'being watched'. This echoes Wheatley's observation that, 'the very presence of CCTV in people's everyday lives, drawn attention to by the real crime genre, suggests that we are not only being protected but also watched' (2001: 49).

· NEW TECHNOLOGIES, FAMILIAR IMAGES ·

Though back in 1984, then, this CCTV technology was (relatively speaking) 'new', its critics argued that the fascination and constraints it held were anything but. In these aspects, the structures and appeal of the medium were not so much inventive as regressive. The role and use of CCTV in contemporary society echoes nothing more than Jeremy Bentham's infamous eighteenth-century model of the *'panopticon'*, the ultimate surveillance building whose enduring citation in analyses of the operation of surveillance is testimony to its powerful and discomforting vision. The panopticon is designed with a central tower housing the supervisor at its core, surrounded by a ring of cells facing out onto the tower whose occupants can always be seen but can not tell whether at any time they are being watched from the tower. Foucault describes it thus: 'They are like so many cages, so many small theatres, in which each actor is alone, perfectly individualised and constantly visible. The panoptic mechanism arranges spatial unities that make it possible to see constantly and to recognise immediately ... Visibility is a trap' (Foucault, 1991: 200).

The continuities borne out here between the panopticon and CCTV seem eerily prophetic. CCTV, with its framing, focusing, zooming and panning capabilities arranges its own 'spatial unities' – as we saw above, Tim Miller describes how the zoom renders the action 'in a way just seeing it happen wouldn't be'. Potentially recording and/or being monitored 24 hours a day, like the panopticon, CCTV's powers of 'recognition' are also constant. Furthermore, in many instances, like the panopticon's central ever-evident tower, the vigilant CCTV camera is visible. Like the panopticon's tower, we can never be certain when CCTV is or isn't staffed, when it may or may not be focusing on us, and hence we must act in its presence at all times as if we are being watched. Where CCTV cameras *aren't* always visible, this makes their inspection of us even more 'unverifiable' than the panopticon. This sense of the simultaneous absence/presence of a remote but powerful sentinel is shared by both forms of surveillance, each raising questions about what we perceive to be the fundamental human right to the dignities borne of privacy. Indeed, the same contentious issues about how the enactment of constant surveillance upon individuals undermines our humanity and human dignity have been at the hub of media debates about reality TV 'game-docs' such as *Big Brother*.

In an intriguing parallel to the panopticon, there was controversy in the United States in 2000 when the first live web-broadcast from a jail went online on Crime.com, a site started by the co-founder of the US reality crime show, *Cops*. A report in the British newspaper *Metro* directly invoked the parallels between this venture and surveillance-based reality TV shows, describing how,

> Getting jailed at the Madison Street Jail in Maricopa County, Phoenix, can make you a star – a star in a rather twisted webcam drama that turns the inside of a county jail into a worldwide *Big Brother* cum-soap opera freakshow for anyone who cares to log on ... Since July last year, the jail's four security cameras have provided live images of the men's and women's holding cells, the search area and the pre-intake area. (Anon, 2001: 41)

Prison reform groups were quick to point out the dubious legality of such broadcasting where people's images were being transmitted without their consent and very often without their knowledge. Nevertheless, this curious venture underlines the enduring potency of a number of the issues raised by the panopticon: our right to privacy, whether criminal behaviour should result in the loss of such rights and our fascination with looking at criminality in its endless shapes and forms.

Foucault's work on the panopticon has been widely adopted in critiques of contemporary surveillance (e.g. Leishman and Mason, 2003), where CCTV has been conceptualised as bearing out his bleak vision of a post-nineteenth-century society managed by the spectre of discipline.[2] But, arguably, CCTV represents the assimilation of aspects of the penal systems that *both* precede and succeed this transitional period. To elucidate, the project of

Foucault's *Discipline and Punish* charts the shifts in the penal systems of the West over some three centuries. This transformation is most evident in the move from pre-nineteenth-century punishment – characterised by the spectacle of public torture (like the 'public hangings' Woffinden's comparative critique of *Crimewatch* evoked above) – to post-nineteenth-century discipline, engendered through surveillance and imprisonment. Foucault describes this as a move from punishment of the body to punishment of the soul. The once huge public events that accompanied executions as massive crowds gathered at the gallows and roadsides, and the public inspection of and participation in all manner of gross tortures visited on the accused's body, now came to an end. By the end of this transitional period, 'Punishment had gradually ceased to be a spectacle. And whatever theatrical elements it still retained were now downgraded' (Foucault, 1991: 9).

We saw above the unnerving ease with which CCTV can be seen to form a parallel with the panopticon and the notion of discipline through surveillance. But the use of CCTV in crime appeals, and later across various reality TV formats, also seems to prolong the pre-nineteenth-century sensibility of spectacle, of 'insatiable curiosity' (Foucault, 1991: 46) in being able to *see* the criminal (a sensibility also evident in the recurrent circulation of photographs of criminals). Where we can't witness their *punishment*, we are nevertheless still fascinated by seeing *them*. The 'nice boys' robbing another youth on a train platform in Willesden in February 2000; the 'Granddad Gang' in March 2000 who rob a petrol station while one of them causes a distraction in the aisle; the April 2000 'woman on a spending spree' with a stolen credit card captured obliviously on film in a shop; all of these are examples of the many instances of CCTV footage where, in every edition, *Crimewatch* serves up the spectacle of CCTV. Shaming is intrinsic to this, something made explicit on *America's Most Wanted*, where CCTV and video footage of the wanted which can be viewed on their website is shown under the banner '15 Seconds of Shame'. Furthermore, the programme also sends its cameras out to record fugitives actually being apprehended and witnesses their arrival at the airport when they are accompanied back to face charges, having been caught on the run; clearly 'identification' is not the purpose here. Rather than the enthralled

'mob' on the street, then, we have the attentive television audience. Rather than the spectacle of gross public torture and
punishment, spectacular display now focuses on seeing the performance of the crime and in identification and/or apprehension
of the criminal. Public and spectacular fascination is nevertheless
at the core of both scenarios, where the 'theatrical elements'
Foucault spoke of persist in the extravagant narratives and con-
frontations seen in some CCTV footage, and where the display
and inspection of the criminal *still* 'deploy[s] its pomp in public'
(Foucault, 1991: 49).

Programmes, such as *Rat Trap* and *SWAG*, which actually construct scenarios that facilitate crime so that their cameras can
catch the wrong-doers on tape, are particularly pertinent here.
They take great pleasure in 'naming and shaming' quite outside
the crime appeal's typical rationale, which is to identify wrong-
doers in order to make an arrest. Indeed the shaming is the punishment here. In one episode of *Rat Trap* (tx 9 January 2000)
looking at the problem of fare dodgers operating out of London's
Cannon Street station, for example, a 'city banker' who, we are
told, was subsequently convicted and fined for fare evasion nevertheless has his face highlighted on screen. The particular
'shame' implicit here is the suggestion that even with a well-paid
and respectable job he tried to swindle the system. Mixing real
crime with *Candid Camera*-style revelation (the hidden camera
format constituting a major generic precursor to the reality TV
movement (Clissold: 2004)), *SWAG* goes a step further, in that its
stated purpose is specifically to expose and embarrass wrong-
doers. As presenter Jason Freeman put it in his opening introduction to one show (tx 6 July 2004): 'Welcome to SWAG, the hidden
camera show that turns the tables on the opportunists and scallies
of this fine nation. We're back for another round of ritual humili-
ation for all those who think they're above and beyond the law.'
In one regular set-up that follows, a lorry filled with expensive
electrical items is left unattended with the back doors wide open.
A woman climbs in, presumably to help herself to the goods, but
as she turns round the back doors close, locking her in, while the
tarpaulin sides of the lorry are rolled back to reveal that she is now
trapped behind bars beneath a banner bearing the programme's
title logo. The lorry is then driven around with her in full view to

parade her guilt. There's more: 'If she thinks being driven through her neighbourhood is all the punishment she'll get, wait till she arrives at *SWAG*'s very own kangaroo court'. At this point she is driven to a warehouse where the programme's own 'judge and jury' find her guilty.

This delight, not merely in catching people in the act, but in parading their faces and inviting audiences and onlookers to laugh at them for having been so spectacularly caught out, reminds one again of another historical precedent – the stocks, where the community once jeered and pelted those guilty of minor misdemeanours. The programme does not touch on the legal implications of its 'evidence'; convictions are not mentioned. This is a space where punishment is enacted, it would seem, purely through the processes of being seen and shamed. As such it mirrors the movement Palmer has identified, evident both in the evolution of 'Judge TV' and the practice of real courtroom judges in the USA, where 'In some states, shaming penalties rather than more traditional punishments are being imposed, with judges recommending that those found guilty should not take up expensive jail space but instead must don signs indicating the nature of the their crimes to the community' (2003: 62–3). He notes that, by showing the faces of criminals caught on tape, *America's Dumbest Criminals* similarly enacts this ritual of 'extending shame' where, like *Rat Trap* and *SWAG*, programme makers (and audiences) do not deem having been found 'Guilty' in court as necessarily constituting the only appropriate punishment.

· AUDIENCES AND THE APPEAL OF ACTUALITY ·

However, as we've seen, despite fears about the potential abuse of CCTV its popularisation, unlike the panopticon, was swift. As the quality of (some) videos increased, they became an essential staple of crime appeal programmes and, indeed, their efficacy seemed impressive; the former producer of *Crime Monthly*, Stewart Morris, claimed that an average of 80% of criminals shown on video were arrested within days of the programme being aired (cited in Campbell, 1993a: 2). Schlesinger and Tumber rightly note that *Crimewatch*'s use of videofits and video footage are 'part of a long journalistic tradition in which pictorial forms of representation have always been an audience-building technique' (1995: 259). Yet this era and its technology undeniably brought new ramifications to bear on the scopophilic pleasure in the image of the criminal. Indeed, as Schlesinger and Tumber observe elsewhere, *Crimewatch* is credited in Britain with having made a breakthrough in the realism of the representation of criminal suspects since it was responsible for developing the 'videofit' (1993: 24–5). By drawing on computer technology it was able to erase the distracting lines and joins between features, which had until this point been characteristic in 'photofits' (as seen in *Police 5*, for example). Dismissed as a 'televisual decoration' in 1984 (Woolley, 1984: 10), the videofit surpassed these origins and the specificity of this medium, enjoying widespread use in criminal appeals where witnesses were able to offer a description. Though the videofit was motivated by the desire for greater verisimilitude, CCTV stills and footage surpassed it again in offering a privileged relationship with realism and authenticity absent both from videofit images and artist's impressions. In this quest for absolute realism, CCTV and video footage is able to transport the viewer into the scene of the crime and, while it is not generally seen 'live' by the audience (O. J. Simpson's motorway police chase being a notable exception, see Bondebjerg, 1995) nevertheless it carries a sense of immediacy and privileged access that reconstructions can not hope to produce.

Interestingly, though, and in apparent contradiction to Stewart Morris above, *Crimewatch* series producer Katie Thomson commented that although sometimes excellent quality footage is shown ('And it's so clear, you think, "We've got him"') nevertheless the expansion of CCTV *'hasn't* enormously increased our success rate. And we show a lot of it. But a lot of it's dreadful quality, a lot of CCTV you think, God, it's hardly worth having a camera there. It's all blurry and set in such dreadful positions' (2002). Here (like Simon Davies from Privacy International cited above), Thomson explodes the myth of CCTV as an unprecedented crime deterrent. Indeed, some criminals have claimed that the poor-quality CCTV footage they witnessed on *Crimewatch* actually gave them an incentive to commit crime. Criminologist

Martin Gill's interviews with 341 imprisoned 'raiders' found that they argued that watching the programme 'showed them how "easy" it was' and highlighted how 'the quality of security film was so poor suspects were difficult to identify' (Burrell, 2000: 7). In fact, this also points to a contradictory aspect of CCTV: that while it enjoys a privileged relationship with the real, it simultaneously holds a distancing quality. The blurry images common to so much CCTV material can make its figures into screen ghosts on occasion. CCTV footage, then, can be both 'real' in content and un-/sur-real in its rendering. As Dovey observes, 'Compared to, say, a 35mm slide the resolution and discernible detail from a surveillance camera is appalling' (2000: 66). From this we can conjecture that the concomitant reason that much CCTV footage is shown is not so much the resounding quality of the image, as its popularity among audiences. This suggests again its peculiarly complex place in contemporary television's evoking of 'the real', where 'the power, significance and 'truthfulness' of surveillance images have embedded themselves in the cultural body' (Dovey, 2000).

Thomson made a particularly thought-provoking observation in interview; that ultimately, no crime appeal *has* to include CCTV or video footage. So, for example, in January 2000, one short *Crimewatch* appeal shows some video footage of a wanted man filmed on a boat on holiday in Torquay. He had pretended to befriend a disabled man he met there, then robbed him. The picture quality is excellent but there is no sound; instead the footage has been overlaid with the sound of the man's voice taken from a different recording. There is absolutely no need, then, to show the moving image since it isn't even synched to the sound. It is all largely superfluous since they could make the same appeal to identify the suspect by merely showing only the clearest (still) image taken from the footage. The use of video here demonstrates how more than mere identification is at stake in the crime appeal's use of the moving image. As Thomson commented, 'That's what *Crimewatch* used to do, just show the best [still] image. But you know, ... it is fair to help people be entertained at the same time'. It is included, then, because audiences enjoy (and indeed now expect) to see it; 'Obviously people like watching CCTV. It's the real thing, especially if it's an action piece. On

CCTV it's quite exciting and again it's making this point *that it is real*' (Thomson, 2002, my emphasis). In short, the use of CCTV conspicuously enhances the programme's claims to authenticity and underlines its sense of a privileged relationship with real crime and actuality, something that programme makers evidently believe to be a ratings winner.

· THE AFFECTIVE POWER OF CCTV IN THE CRIME APPEAL ·

Series producer Tim Miller from *Britain's Most Wanted* made a very similar observation to Thomson's above. He spoke with tangible enthusiasm about the televisual drama of CCTV footage and thus its crucial place in his programme. In his words,

> Actuality is the most dramatic thing you can have, because it's real. That's why the show's been quite successful, isn't it really, people like watching real stuff. It's real actuality but not in real time, because you don't have to wait for the incident to unfold ... you just get the punch-line of each one. (T. Miller, 2001)

Interestingly, what Miller points to here is a post-modern, Baudrillardan sense of CCTV as a kind of super-*enhanced* realism, as being 'more real than real'. Similarly, Hill's work on *Coppers*, a programme where a camera crew shadows real-life police at work, bears this out. She describes how one episode details the humdrum series of petty crimes that police work through in Southend-on-Sea. Viewers expecting thrills and drama because it's about real crime will be disappointed; 'This is real-life and real life is not always exciting'. Like the crime appeal and its use of CCTV, *Coppers* is about 'real' crime, but where CCTV is recurrently used as a form of spectacular display, *Coppers* is about the 'ordinariness of crime'. Another episode, for example, shows divers on the Thames discovering a body, something one might expect to be rather dramatic. But instead, 'We see how long it takes ... how awkward it is ... and how cold everyone gets waiting for the procedure to be over' (Annette Hill, 2000: 230–1). Through its *edited* packaging on crime appeal programmes, CCTV footage eliminates precisely this sense of 'waiting; or 'dead' time'. Through

CCTV the audience can actually experience a heightened sense of realism; they don't have to go through any superfluous narrative or, in Miller's words, 'wait for the incident to unfold'. What CCTV enables them to get is pure adrenalin, the moment of high drama, 'the punch-line' and the pleasure it offers audiences is inextricably bound up in this.

But crucially, the genre does not just provide these visual records and representations of *criminals*. Again, this fact underlines how the genre's fascination with looking and seeing, with privileged access to actuality evidence and with the visual records that accompany crime stories, is not only, nor primarily, about identifying the perpetrators of crime. As we saw in Chapter 3 on photography, for *Crimewatch* series producer Katie Thomson, the use of videos and photos of victims is crucial to the programme's sense of realism. I want to return again to her thoughts here, in order to explore the light they shed on the use of *moving image* material of victims. Thomson commented:

> I think it's always about reminding people that this has happened to a real person, especially when you see so much crime drama, this *is* about real people ... We're always trying to say these are real lives we're talking about, this isn't an interesting reconstruction, this is a real person or family that's been destroyed. And home video helps a lot with that, because I think that has a real impact. It makes people feel this person was moving and walking and talking and enjoying a birthday party six months ago and now they're dead. (2002)

There are two notions that Thomson alludes to here that are particularly interesting and worth further consideration. Firstly, she immediately seeks to contextualise tragedy by placing the victim within the context of bereaved *families*. As we have seen, the principal way that *Crimewatch* continually positions and legitimises its victims is within their familial context(s); *Crimewatch* victims are never merely or primarily individuals, but parents, children, siblings, spouses. Secondly, Thomson suggests that home videos, and indeed CCTV footage, of the victim are even more effective and affective in their impact on the viewer than photos; there is something potent about seeing the victim 'moving and walking and talking' that moves the audience in ways the still image can not. This forms a parallel with the way in which, as we have seen, programme makers believe CCTV (i.e. moving images) of criminals carry more impact than 'mug-shots' or stills. There is something about seeing the criminal 'moving and walking and talking' on CCTV that make it the more compelling media, just as real footage of the victim seen living and breathing gives it a power that stills do not have.

In all this we can identify how an affective conjunction is at work in the crime appeal's use of video technologies. This lies in the manner in which its *illusion of immediacy* converges with the fact of its *'this-has-been'-ness*. In this latter description I again paraphrase Roland Barthes's words on the nature of photography and, as we saw in the last chapter, his account of how every photo is ineluctably bound up in its own past tense (1993: 77). It is a term that bears potent application to the visual media of CCTV and video too. In fact, this conjunction, this conflictual or paradoxical meeting of present and past tenses is arguably at its most affective in CCTV or home-video footage of the *victim*, since here its 'this-has-been'-ness is intensified by the fact of their death; we must acknowledge that the person so alive before us, 'moving and walking and talking' on our screens, will never do any of these things again. A particularly powerful instance of this is seen in April 2000, in the first anniversary reconstruction of the murder of *Crimewatch* presenter, Jill Dando. Dando's cousin tells how the most traumatic aspect of dealing with the coverage of her murder was seeing the footage of Dando shopping in the high-street electrical store Dixons, just minutes before she drove home and was murdered. She describes how, 'The worst thing was seeing the film clip of Jill's last moments ... and the fact that you do just want to be able to stop the camera and stop the action and to shout out at her and say "Jill, don't go home!"' Here, footage of a victim caught unawares by CCTV in a mundane and everyday act – the purchase of a printer cartridge – is transformed, retrospectively, into a potent and affecting spectacle. As we cut back to the studio, presenter Nick Ross comments blithely, 'Amen. If only the tape could be rewound', as if the properties of time itself were contained within or controlled by the medium – a comment that underlines my argument that CCTV holds a peculiarly affective relationship with our perceptions of the operation of temporality. The affective power of CCTV footage evoked by Dando's cousin in her appeal to the screen crystallises what I have described about the operation of the medium; how it both draws the viewer in with the illusion of immediacy (she describes wanting to address the screen as if the 'action' was live) and demands that the viewer embrace its 'this-has-been'-ness (she must accept the futility of her desire to 'stop' time, since the time of the film is past).

A similar poignancy is drawn on in the appeal, discussed in Chapter 3, regarding Emma Caldwell's murder (tx June 2005). After the interview with her parents has established the context in which she had become a drug addict and prostitute, we are shown real CCTV footage of her leaving her hostel the night she disappeared and then walking along the street outside. There is nothing of interest to see here; quite the reverse, it is even more ordinary in content that Dando's shopping expedition since the victim here is not even a celebrity. But it is retrospectively rendered compelling; there is the same sense of terrible poignancy in seeing these last captured images of the victim, knowing as we do, now, and as she could not have, then, that within a short time of her leaving that hostel she would be murdered. John Ellis has argued that it is *cinema* which is 'profoundly marked by what Roland Barthes has called the "photo effect"', a quality he defines as 'the paradox that the photograph presents an absence that is present' (Ellis, 1994: 58, 93). But in *Crimewatch* we see that, through its incorporation of CCTV, domestic video and still photography, television too can affectively co-opt 'the photo-effect'. Ellis comments that the 'photo effect of present absence can produce an almost *intolerable nostalgia*' (1994: 58, my italics). His evocative phrase entirely mirrors the angst summoned up by *Crimewatch*'s painful reprise of the visual documenting of the now-dead in its CCTV and video footage; the 'present absence', in fact, of the murder victim.

· CAUGHT IN THE ACT – THE REAL CRIME CLIPSHOW ·

So far this chapter has evidenced that whether it is in the dramatic scenes of a robbery in process, or a victim in their final hours unknowingly going about the mundane business of everyday life, our ongoing absorption with CCTV footage pivots on the spectacle of actuality. I want now to turn to another real crime format that similarly pivots on the use of CCTV and other video surveillance footage; the 'clipshow' programme.

Annette Hill's audience research on reality TV found *Police Camera Action!* to be enormously popular, attracting audiences of 13.2 million in 1994 (2005: 26) and belonging to the 'police/ crime' group of reality programmes watched most widely in 2000 'either regularly or occasionally by 72% of adults and 71% of children' (2005: 3). The programme is characterised by Hill, like *Crimewatch*, as 'infotainment' (2005: 26). But, like *Crimewatch* too, its claims to having been primarily prompted by the desire to offer 'information' to the public is somewhat tenuous. The programme consists in the main of montages of clips provided by police constabularies from around the UK, taken from traffic and motorway cameras, police cars and helicopters, showing the dangerous and illegal behaviour of some drivers and, typically, the ways in which police apprehend them. The presenter, popular newscaster Alastair Stewart, filmed the 'links' between clips at apt venues which, with police assistance, in some instances included police premises. While a press officer at the Metropolitan Police, I sometimes worked on the filming of these links to facilitate the camera crew at work (this included those outlined in the episode examined here, tx 20 December 1996, filmed at the Met Police's Air Support Unit in Lippetts Hill and their driver training school at Hendon). The fact that police co-operate with such programme makers, not merely by providing video material but by giving them the time, staff and access to film links at their facilities and training venues, is a marker of the interest police hold in shows like *Police Camera Action!*

In part, this is a commercial interest; the clips sold provide a source of income, albeit minor. But beyond this, their co-operation arguably suggests that the police believe that these programmes show them in a positive and sympathetic light, demonstrating just some of the precarious situations they must manage daily and the various means open to them to help achieve this. *Police Camera Action!* shows police dealing professionally with difficult and dangerous situations, having mastery over some impressive technology, ensuring justice is done and, most importantly for the themes of this chapter, as having access to a ubiquitous range of surveillance technology. In this way, like the crime appeal programme, the real crime clipshow might be accused of being complicit in serving the interests of the police. Hence Palmer has argued that action-based police footage programmes such as *Police Camera Action!* both reflect and contribute to an evolving discursive formation 'which has changed how we are governed and what we are invited to understand as *good governance*', with an emphasis on improving security rather than promoting debate (2003: 44). At the same time, this format very much serves the interests of programme makers too, looking to create affordable but action-charged popular TV. Clips lend themselves to recycling; for example, one episode of *Tarrant on CCTV* (tx 1 August 2005) included two extracts seen in the opening credit montage sequence of *World's Wildest Police Videos* (where a drunk driver dances with a traffic cone on his head and a patrol officer issuing a ticket narrowly misses death when another driver ploughs into the back of the car he's just pulled over). They were shown at greater length, but nevertheless have clearly been in circulation on TV for some years.

However, the tone and content of Stewart's commentary in *Police Camera Action!* is essential to how we might try to grasp the objectives, purpose and pleasures of the programme more fully, be these openly acknowledged by the programme makers or otherwise. Close analysis reveals it to have multiple levels of address, which speak of the different and possible conflicting interests at work in the programme. *Police Camera Action!* is, on the one hand, as Hill's 'infotainment' categorisation suggests, superficially interested in demonstrating police work, their techniques and technologies, whilst it also takes a 'public service' slant at times in issuing advice and reminders about safe driving. 'Never try to retrieve anything that you've dropped on the motorway, however precious or potentially dangerous!' Stewart tells us following footage of a lorry driver who tried to gather up a dropped load of nails; 'Unsafe loads are an accident waiting to happen!' he warns, after one lazy driver fails to use a tarpaulin and his belongings start to fly off the back of his truck. We might also say it 'informs' in a rather repressive sense, guided by the desire to curtail censurable behaviour in the viewing public, in that it underlines quite unambiguously how the police surveil public space continually. (There are a 'growing number of police video cars on the road today' Stewart notes somewhat ominously at the very start of the programme).

For example, in a lengthy link midway through this episode, as a prologue to aerial footage of a fleeing car thief and a 'hidden' intruder, who both light up like white beacons on the screen when filmed by helicopters fitted with thermal imaging cameras, Stewart first talks through the technology and its powers. With the help of a Met Police helicopter at the Lippetts Hill Air Support Unit, he demonstrates how the camera is heat- rather than light-sensitive as he walks towards it in the dark and suddenly becomes visible when the thermal imaging camera replaces the standard camera. 'So, even in the dark', he explains, 'police can follow their target wherever it goes. And from the ground, there's no way of knowing when the camera's being used'. The scopic reach of the police is indeed expansive here and his words and tone, with their implicit warning-cum-threat, are arguably meant to be something of a deterrent. (Indeed, the fascination of this thermal imaging technology persists a decade later, forming some of the most compelling material in more recent real crime shows featuring police clips such as *Traffic Cops* (BBC, tx 28 July 2005)). There is also no ambiguity about the legal repercussions of having one's bad driving or unlawful activities caught on film and the status of such 'evidence' as a marker of truth; in a later link, as a policeman pops a tape into an evidence bag and locks it away, Stewart informs us, 'almost without exception, the tapes in these vaults will convict the driver in question, no matter how much he or she continues to protest their innocence' – a sentiment that once again serves to justify the ubiquity of surveillance cameras.

But this is also a programme that takes great and barely concealed delight in the *spectacle of actuality* again; it holds up for our amusement, our horror and our amazement the outrageous, dangerous and foolish behaviour of 'other' people. The very title of the programme, *Police Camera Action!*, situates it in the tradition of cinematic-style spectacle and acknowledges its performance qualities. Stewart's commentary is sometimes serious, always disapproving, often haughty; but it is also at times facetious, teasing and – like the guides who provided voiceover explanations to early cinema – *revelatory*. Scenes of a hitchhiker improbably and insistently trying to get a lift on a motorway by walking out in front of cars, end with Stewart drolly noting that 'this impatient young man' did 'finally get a lift – in the back of a police patrol car'. In another comical aside, following scenes of a motorcyclist illegally pulling a trailer containing his dog behind him, Stewart observes, 'He may be your best friend, but he won't be able to help you if you get pulled over by the police'. He as good as tells us to brace ourselves for a bumpy ride before one montage of clips, by trailing it with the titillating words, 'some people do the craziest things'. Alongside the programme's serious, censuring, surveilling warnings, then, are ample opportunities and invitations to take a moment's decadent pleasure in the illegal and dangerous activities of the people captured on film here.

In one sequence, a motorcyclist tries to remain balanced as a 10-foot plank horizontally attached to the bike's rear wobbles precariously. Admitting that the sequence has been widely seen and disseminated before, Stewart comments, 'This clip from Liverpool is legendary ... but badly loaded vehicles are no laughing matter'. This remark precisely reveals the real tension between what is overtly voiced (the superficial 'lesson' at stake) and what is nevertheless actually happening here; which is that, despite the show's ostensibly 'serious' intentions, clearly the audience will be laughing at the sheer absurdity of this motorcyclist. Its comedy value is precisely the reason the clip has been shown despite it already being 'legendary'; indeed, that is what has *made* it legendary. Working its way through one shocking clip after another, all the while reminding us that this is real footage captured by the powers of (ever-emergent) video surveillance technologies, *Police Camera Action!* sometimes echoes in part the principles of Tom Gunning's 'cinema of attractions' (1990), where early cinema audiences would be amazed by the images, and by the technology itself, of the new medium of filmmaking; it similarly hails us to expect to be astonished by what we're about to see.

Arguably, then, *Police Camera Action!*, and subsequent programmes of its kind such as *World's Wildest Police Videos*, are not merely cautionary and censorious, a tone the programme makers arguably feel obliged to adopt in order to protect themselves somewhat from accusations of being wholly exploitative or salacious. They are also arguably in part *celebratory* of 'counter-cultural' or non-conformist behaviour in that they offer up its spectacle for our entertainment, taking pleasure in its excess, however mediated by an intermittently censuring commentary. As Biressi and Nunn note,

> Since the 1990s new reality genres of crime and emergency services programming have appeared. These rely even more heavily on amateur, CCTV or police footage to present a montage of criminality and emergency services drama and, unlike law and order programming, *they make little claim to help prevent or solve crime*. (2005: 120, my italics)

In this respect, these programmes are perhaps less disingenuous about some of their less civic-minded intentions than crime appeal programmes, where the public service justification for their use of CCTV is writ far larger. Since the demise of *Crimestoppers* and *Crime Monthly*, real crime clipshows have also in some respects replaced the prevalence of the crime appeal format in British schedules. This shift might be said to indicate that the cultural climate is changing and that programme makers, while not abandoning a 'public service' rationale, feel less pressurised to offer it than they once did in some of their real crime programming.

Biressi and Nunn go on to argue, however, that these newer formats nevertheless overwhelmingly retain an 'ideological framework' that adopts 'moral discourses of criminal justice', privileging a 'single indisputable reading of events' rather than opening up the possibility of a critique of the law (2005: 122). Similarly, Palmer suggests that programmes like *Police Camera Action!*, *Cops* and *Real Stories of the Highway Patrol* serve a propagandist function for the police, endorsing their role as 'authoritarian agents of criminal control' in such a manner that they 'work to close down meaning' (2003: 59, 66). For Palmer, these programmes have a didactic impulse; 'The new emphasis is a *practical* one; how we should behave and how we expect others to behave' (2003: 17). The notion that *Police Camera Action!* and its compatriots seek to impart a 'message' also emerged in Annette Hill's audience research, where she found young male respondents reflected on 'how the programme can teach people "that you shouldn't do stuff like that"' (2005: 102). But equally she found that they joked about it teaching them how to drive 'at 130 miles an hour and not go into anything' and also that they were alert to how only positive police stories were selected for the programme (Annette Hill, 2005: 103). In other words, despite Palmer's fear that these programmes 'close down meaning', we can see a variety of responses evident in Hill's respondents, from 'subversive' pleasure in learning about illegal behaviour, to awareness of the show's serious 'message' about police surveillance, to a critical consciousness of the ramifications of the programme's selectivity.

While acknowledging the presence of the framework that Palmer (2003) and Biressi and Nunn (2005) identify, then, I would argue that this 'moral discourse' often appears unconvincing, trite and superficial, an obligatory nod to culturally approved values, and that these programmes frequently embrace the pleasures of anticipation, excitement and spectacle of scenes of dissension rather more enthusiastically than their endorsement of law and order. In this respect, structurally they echo the gangster movies of 1930s Hollywood or *The Jerry Springer Show* in the 1990s (the confessional talk show constituting another prime instance of the tabloidisation of TV in this period). Both were equally obliged to end on an openly moral or edifying note in order to mount some 'defence' for their having exhibited such deviant excesses. Similarly, going back further still in the history of true crime to the publication of the first *Newgate Calendar* in 1773, Biressi found that the agenda of this respectable, five-volume edition of true crime stories was 'ostensibly one of moral instruction'. Nevertheless, she also found that, then, like now, its 'edification is tempered with entertainment'. Furthermore, opening up the possibility of a more polysemic reception, its violent tales 'could also (albeit inadvertently) *glorify the criminal who refuses to capitulate*' (Biressi, 2001: 48–50, my italics).

World's Wildest Police Videos (*WWPV*), the US equivalent of *Police Camera Action!*, does not attempt to adopt quite the same tone of 'public service' information in its commentary; the programme makes very little pretence of contextualising the 'lessons' of its police footage with tips on safe driving or crime prevention advice. Instead it adopts a louder, brasher, more unrelenting voiceover, courtesy of Sheriff John Bunnell, repeatedly hammering home the madness of the dangerous drivers whom we are watching, the absolute necessity of apprehending them, and the calamitous consequences that could result from their behaviour. In the lengthy credit sequence (series tx on 5, 2003) we open with an extended montage of crashes, chases and fights, accompanied by the following startling introduction from Bunnell:

> Look around. No matter where you are, at any second it could happen to you. Because desperate criminals use desperate measures, no matter who gets in the way. For the next 60 minutes, you'll get a close-up view of what officers see every day. You'll ride shotgun in the most terrifying chases on the road. You'll feel the heat of the most explosive acts of criminal insanity ever captured on tape. Much of this footage has never been viewed by the public. Police and news agencies send us their most shocking videos, so that you can know what they know; that to let your guard down, even for an instant, could mean disaster. So crank up your TV and don't turn away, because real life happens in the blink of an eye.

A number of interesting ideas are foregrounded here; we are excitedly promised that we are about to have *privileged* access to footage not seen by the ordinary public before, astonishing material we will experience in 'close-up'. We will witness authentic 'real life' incidents, positioning us vicariously as/with the police themselves ('what officers see every day'). But we are also in no doubt from Bunnell's opening remarks that in *WWPV*, the police – and by extension the community – are consistently under attack from a bewildering array of utterly reckless, and highly determined, criminally dangerous drivers. Safety and security are precarious states in the world of *WWPV*, they could shatter 'in the blink of an eye'. The frenetic pace and tone of the voiceover throughout the programme, accompanied by a constant soundtrack of collisions, sirens wailing and tyres screeching, functions to endorse the necessity of police retaliation; faced with such mayhem, if any of us are to be safe, 'The only way to fight back against this kind of force is to take the offensive' (tx 9 November 2003). Criminals are spoken about in unrelentingly contemptuous terms – 'This small-time thug has become another big-time loser' – while police officers are selflessly 'working non-stop to make sure criminals pay for their crime'.

In the same episode, when one speeding driver is finally pulled over, it is discovered that his baby son is in the rear of the car. Bunnell's voiceover is incredulous; 'They can't believe a man would be so careless with his own son's life!' We hear the police ask why he didn't stop, to which he replies simply, as he lies on the floor with a gun pointing at him, 'Scared'. But any engagement with or exploration of why this man might genuinely have been fearful to find himself the subject of a police check is glossed over. Instead we return quickly to Bunnell's dismay about the man's irresponsible parenting, which apparently compounds his criminal status: 'He was more worried about getting caught than he was about his own child!' As such, the discourse of *WWPV* does indeed seem to demonstrate Palmer's concerns that such programming can have a repressive function, rousing public support for, and delimiting debate about, police authority by portraying a world in which police, faced with a seemingly endless stream of car thieves and drunk drivers, consistently risk life and limb 'to protect and serve'. The sheer might of the police force in relation to criminals is also frequently stressed. In one sequence a drunk driver who won't get out of his car has 'nine officers physically tear him away' (tx on 5, 16 November 2003); in another incident, after one officer in pursuit drives into a tree and a number of other patrol vehicles take over, Bunnell notes 'Suspects who run from the law don't always realise, when an officer runs into trouble he's got back-up and the chase goes on. But when a crook makes a mistake, he's done' (tx on 5, 23 November 2003). Debate about this heavy deployment of resources is, of course, absent.

But if the terms of *WWPV*'s reactionary, admonishing voiceover are proportionally more insistent than *Police Camera Action!*'s, so too is its delight in the spectacle of its footage. The credits open with an onscreen warning (also used by *Cops*) that holds the same enticing promise of forbidden fruits as an R18 certificate; 'Due to the graphic nature of this programme, viewer discretion is advised'. As noted above, what follows is an 80-second montage of gunfire, cars crashing, tyres blowing, rioting, and trucks careering off the road, which wouldn't look out of place in a Hollywood blockbuster. The voiceover may well seem ominous and paranoid in tone as, in heavy-handed fashion, we are informed 'it could happen' to any of us. But combined as it is with such a frenetic, exhilarating series of visuals, there is little chance that this sequence could be mistaken for 'a gritty public service announcement', as Palmer has said of *Police Camera Action!* (2003: 65), particularly not as it ends with an invitation to 'crank up [our] TV'. Like Gunning's cinema of attractions again, what follows is going to be more like a trip to the fairground. Indeed, adopting language that would be at home in an amusement park, Sheriff Bunnell promises in his opening prologue that we're about to 'ride shotgun' and ends his first link, having climbed into a police car, by telling us, 'So buckle up – it's going to be a fast ride!' His language situates what we're about to undergo as a physical, sensory experience; we will watch in 'close-up', 'ride shotgun', 'feel the heat'. The evident fascination these programmes demonstrate with the sheer excess and vitality of criminal behaviour (repeatedly shown in multiple takes, with slo-mo and close-ups) – even if this exists within a narrative that assures the audience that wrongdoers are apprehended and punished and police authority is unquestioningly validated and revered – means that there are more pleasures to be had, more spectatorial positions to be taken here, than in those programmes that endorse a law and order discourse. Contradictorily, the central allure of the programme, which is explicit rather than implied, comes in its very promise to make us privileged witnesses to the spectacular activities of the very people who do not abide by this discourse.

The concerns that commentators such as Palmer (2003) and Biressi and Nunn (2005) have voiced, then, regarding the manner in which these real crime clipshows (and indeed crime appeal programmes) have helped validate and naturalise contemporary surveillance culture, bear considerable weight. As Biressi and Nunn note, 'reality programmes expand the membership of law enforcement to include supposedly vigilant and supportive televisual citizens whose active interest and "assistance" validates the filming and screening of criminal spectacles', inviting viewers to 'collude in the entrapment of the "criminal"' while disingenuously providing 'vicarious pleasures' under the cover of a 'responsible' agenda (2005: 122). The ethical questions raised by programmes such as *Rat Trap* and *SWAG* – which actually construct the conditions which it is hoped will result in a crime occurring in order to ensure that their cameras are there to capture the moment (e.g. a car left in a known 'smash and grab hotspot' with a bag on the front seat (*Rat Trap*, tx on BBC1, 9 January 2000)) – are particularly troubling. Nevertheless, and while acknowledging the simplistic manner in which these programmes decontextualise crime, we should keep sight of their potential to be read in other, less complicit and more transgressive ways. In real crime clipshows, the spectacular exhibition of the sheer gall, determination and recklessness of criminal behaviour is not the 'side-show' companion to a feature story on police capability, but rather the main attraction.

That debates around the ethics of reality TV have so conspicuously seemed to mimic or renew those earlier associated with the crime appeal format is testimony to how these televisual forms or movements share much common ground – and how there is much in this 'new' trend, like the 'new' technologies of CCTV and video in the 1980s, that is far from new in its attraction. The competitive environment in which television circulates ensures that it must continually develop, revive and adapt its forms and genres. Yet still in recent years, the debates and fears that accompany the arrival of 'new' televisual movements, as we have seen here, seem often to reproduce the same familiar discourses of anxiety about the potential power (and abuse) of television.[3] Thus, misgivings about voyeuristic audiences, sensationalist narratives and the questionable use of surveillance footage were already established features within critical discourses around television in relation to crime appeal programming when they emerged again 15 years later in relation to *Big Brother*. Indeed, so too, for that matter, were anxieties about the exploitation of participants and generic slippage. Undeniably reality TV now constitutes an expansive and distinctive televisual movement in broadcasting history, an unquestionable shift in the make-up of contemporary television schedules; but, as this chapter has argued, the pleasures, curiosities and gratifications that underlie it may not be as original or landmark as we have tended to presume.

· NOTES ·

1 I say *consolidated* since, despite the worthy public service justification for showing such footage on *Crimewatch* – i.e. criminal identification and apprehension – its use was also always, simultaneously, embedded in audience entertainment.
2 Elsewhere, theorists have suggested that the development of the mass media has meant the panopticon has been replaced by the 'synopticon' (where the many observe the few) (see Mathiesen, 1997).
3 Indeed many of the discourses examined and arguments posited here critiquing the reality TV movement would bear application to the emergence of the 'tabloid talk show'.

5 Pleasure, Fear and Fortitude
WOMEN WATCHING *CRIMEWATCH UK*

In this final chapter I present an audience case study of real crime TV, in particular reflecting on the relationship between the crime appeal format and gender, by examining how the female viewer of *Crimewatch* has been constructed. This arena is particularly rich in material, and particularly significant for extending our understanding of the relationship between audiences and real crime TV, given the way that women have consistently featured as the real casualties of fear of crime. Using existing audience research projects, interviews with production personnel, reviews and women's own testimonies drawn from the British press, I look at how *Crimewatch* holds such a significant place in the perceptions of crime, television and fear of crime held by many British women. By looking too at *Crimewatch*'s representation of the female viewer's commonest screen surrogate, the female victim, I examine how the programme promotes a generally ideologically repressive and conservative account of the relationship between gender and violent crime. Women watching *Crimewatch* will rarely see other women featured in any other guise. As producer Belinda Phillips observed; 'Sometimes you get them in "named faces" and occasionally on CCTV', but, on the whole, '[women] do tend to be the victims in *Crimewatch*' (2002).[1]

The potential repercussions of this must not be underestimated given, as noted in Chapter 2, how television has been identified by some research as playing a powerful role in effecting fear of crime, and that fear of crime has been widely understood as a condition to which women are particularly prone to (Stanko, 1992). I argue that the discourses surrounding women as the most vulnerable party in fear-of-crime debates have worked to construct fear of crime as a 'female malady' (Showalter, 2000) bearing many of the hallmarks of that most quintessentially feminine of conditions, *hysteria*. What this stereotype of the paranoid woman overcome by an 'irrational' fear of crime fails to recognise adequately is that women have to rationalise 'real' risk statistics in the face of the media's overwhelming saturation and preoccupation with crimes against women, particularly sex attacks and murders by strangers. This is a context that *Crimewatch* very much contributes to and one that belies the fact that women are actually most at risk from domestic violence and attacks by those known to them (Stanko, 1990). Indeed, Jock Young has argued that the programme is skewed by the fact that, 'it tends to reflect the interests of CID, who are always more attracted to the spectacular, macho crime' (cited in Woffinden, 1989: 11). So, for example, on the other side of the coin, *Crimewatch* also rarely acknowledges 'white-collar crime' such as corporate fraud. Young's observation suggests that in fact the whole show is implicated in a masculine worldview that will offer little innovation on women's relationship with crime. As *Crimewatch* series producer Katie Thomson acknowledged, 'You are most at risk as a male in your late teens. Obviously that would never come over from *Crimewatch*' (2002). This is because the kinds of crime these male victims are most likely to suffer – sudden and swift muggings or assaults in streets and pubs – don't make 'good' television, just as they don't 'reflect the interests of CID'. In Thomson's words, 'There's often not much to show – a street stabbing, there's nothing to reconstruct' (2002). Again we see, then, how the interests of the police and television coincide and feed into a mutually sustained cycle that succeeds in privileging sex attacks against women as one of the most newsworthy of crimes; thus contributing to a climate which perpetuates what Schlesinger et al. have called 'a culture of peril' for women (1992: 63).

Many of my conclusions in this chapter concur with those made by Cavender, Bond-Maupin and Jurik in the US (1999) in their analysis of 'The Construction of Gender in Reality Crime TV', which focused on *America's Most Wanted*. Like them, my analysis finds that in reconstructions 'strangers continue to be over-represented as assailants of adult women'; 'horror movie techniques were used in vignettes to portray women victims'; and 'these narratives reinforce cultural stereotypes about men and women' (Cavender et al., 1999: 653, 656). However, Cavender et al. conclude from this that *America's Most Wanted*'s conservatism is so pervasive that it precludes women viewers from any kind of rewarding or 'transgressive' engagement with these programmes. In contrast, I examine how some women actually appear to use and negotiate these apparently highly conservative frameworks in more oppositional and productive ways. Biressi and Nunn touch briefly on this when they observe, 'it can be argued that the narrativisation of crime in both fact and fictional forms provides a secure container for fear and those things that incite fear – the other, the alien and so on, shaping it and directing it into manageable formations' (2005: 122). Pursuing this in more detail and challenging the prevalent perception of women viewers of real crime TV as being damaged by anxiety, I posit that many women may actually be using the programmes to *confront and manage* their fear of crime.

Indeed, I open by looking at the ways in which despite (and, paradoxically, sometimes *because* of) its often sensationalistic depictions of violent crime against women, *Crimewatch* may nevertheless provide the audience, and the majority female audience especially, with various forms of *pleasure*. The notion of audience 'pleasure' in *Crimewatch* may seem hard to reconcile and it is understandable that there may be some reluctance, by both critics and audiences themselves, to think of it consciously in these terms, given the morbid nature of so much that it deals with. Schlesinger et al., in their audience research with female viewers, seem distinctly uncomfortable in their study when they note that almost half of the women who had 'no experience of violence' rated it as 'entertaining or very entertaining' while a quarter of those 'with experience of violence' did so (1992: 51). Arguably these figures suggest a lot of women *do* find the programme 'entertaining', a fact seemingly underlined by the fact that 69% of their sample were 'occasional' or 'regular' viewers while 65% 'always' or 'sometimes' watched *Crimewatch Update* (Schlesinger et al., 1992: 51). Unsurprisingly perhaps, given the sadistic or masochistic overtones that pleasure in true crime seems to carry, 'pleasure' is an element of *Crimewatch* that has gone almost completely without comment from seemingly discomforted critics. I argue that it is crucial to explore the notion of pleasure in order to understand the show's enduring popularity. And, by reconceptualising the female viewer as an active and critical one, even while acknowledging *Crimewatch*'s contribution to popular culture's ubiquitous fascination with violent crime against women, it is possible to understand her as an agent involved in processing fear of crime rather than merely being its victim.

· TRUE CRIME, REAL PLEASURE ·

It is easy in the face of *Crimewatch*'s recurrent accounts of human loss, and in the face of all the criticisms of real crime TV's dubious taste, to lose sight of the fact that this genre, like any other, brings with it many audience pleasures. The reconstruction of real crime has clearly long carried an attraction for audiences, which the 1980s fear-of-crime debate neglected either to acknowledge fully or to seek to understand. Arguably, pleasures are gained by *Crimewatch* audiences in a variety of ways. For example, the *Women Viewing Violence* researchers (Schlesinger et al., 1992) found that their respondents spoke in enthusiastic and admiring terms about the ingenuity of some of the more resourceful cons perpetrated on *Crimewatch*. This included a gang of robbers/confidence tricksters who had managed to persuade a series of Mercedes drivers to hand over their car keys on the premise of fixing a faked oil leak – unsurprisingly they never saw their cars again – a fact that also led the respondents to talk in quite disparaging terms about the victims.

Again, there are historical precedents for this kind of oppositional reading or valorisation of true crime. Foucault's historical account of the pre-nineteenth-century penal system described how the public's use of and response to public torture and execution was in no way uniformly consensual, since at public punishments the crowds would sometimes turn on the executioner, fights would break out, interventions occur. Furthermore, broadsheets and death-songs released after the trial were instrumental in elevating some criminals to hero status (Foucault, 1991: 60–7). We saw in Chapter 4 how real crime clipshows could be said to enjoy the spectacle of criminal behaviour, even while outwardly condemning it. Similarly, some 200 years after the period discussed by Foucault, we can still see how a sneaking admiration for some resourceful criminals on *Crimewatch* endows them with a kind of respect that flies in the face of concern with 'law and order' politics, and in some ways undermines the discourse of disapproval that the viewer is invited to share. The pleasure here, then, comes partly in uncovering the tactics of the robbers but also in the gullibility of some victims. Though violent crime was always taken seriously by the *Women Viewing Violence* respondents, 'some property offences were seen as amusing or entertaining' and the perpetrators even 'likened to Arthur Daley', the loveable Cockney rogue from the British series *Minder* (Schlesinger et al., 1992: 56–7). Similarly *Britain's Most Wanted* series producer Tim Miller spoke about a memorable theft captured on CCTV, shown on the programme. A fraudster had visited an exclusive jeweller and asked to see a specific diamond ring. During the course of the transaction he swapped it for a near-identical fake he'd had made up (which itself was worth £5,000) then left before anyone realised. Miller described how this crime had '"The Wow Factor". The audience will think, 'That guy's brave' or 'what a great scam'. It's a really professional crime' (2001). Again this suggests audience pleasure in and admiration of criminal ingenuity, rendering them 'anti-heroes', something quite at odds with the predominant discourse of condemnation that crime appeals must typically be seen to have.

Perhaps the closest *Crimewatch* ever comes to humour is in pointing out the absurdity of some criminals. Here the enjoyment lies in the wry commentary on their foolishness where the audience joins the presenter in vaguely amused dismay. For example, in March 2000 a gang of three elderly petrol station thieves are nicknamed the 'Granddad Gang'; building-society robbers who seem oblivious to the CCTV camera perfectly picturing them are 'not the brightest pair'; an over-elaborate, botched assault on a security van that incorporated a boat, van and battering ram is 'one of the most ridiculous attempted robberies in Britain'. The pleasure in spectacle and haughty voiceover here has much in common again with *World's Wildest Police Videos* and *Police Camera Action!* On these occasions, we enjoy a sense of superiority over the criminal and in seeing or hearing about some of the more farcical elements of some criminal endeavours. The genre also sometimes offers pleasure in the *anticipation* of people being caught; if a criminal has allowed themselves to be unambiguously caught in the act on camera, the audience again takes satisfaction from their foolishness and the certainty that they will now be identified. Tim Miller pointed to the gratification this brings the viewer, while also recognising again an aspect of the community appeal of the programme, when he imagined viewers watching and discussing it together; 'If it's a very good image, everybody will be sitting next to their neighbour going "They'll get him". It's a bit like *Mastermind* or something when they know the answer, you know, *you feel part of the programme*' (T. Miller, 2001, my emphasis).

Crimewatch's own audience research has shown that the programme is watched by more women than men (Thomson, 2002) and for this reason it is pertinent to reflect on what the gendered pleasures of the programme may be. Interestingly, *Crimewatch*'s findings contrast with those of Oliver and Armstrong's research into the audience for real crime programmes, including *Cops*, *America's Most Wanted* and *FBI: The Untold Story*. They found that *men* were the predominant audience: 'Aficionados of the true crime shows were overwhelmingly white males with high levels of authoritarianism and racism, who took pleasure in the dramatic arrest footage' (Brenton and Cohen, 2003: 40). What this perhaps points to is that women may well be more drawn to the reconstruction narratives of real crime programming than other action-led, fast-paced, 'actuality' formats. Here, we might speculate whether the reconstruction programmes do more to attend to what are traditionally seen as 'female' interests and skills – reading people, witnessing, talking – all of which bring to mind the pleasures of *soaps* for the female audience (see Geraghty, 1991). While being wary of making merely essentialist interpretations of audience tastes, it may be that women prefer reconstruction programmes for their interest in providing 'a social history' (Cavender and Bond-Maupin, 1993: 308), for their emphasis on *story* over narrative *climax* (the arrest, the collision, the surrender and so on) that are the foci of other real crime formats. In this respect it is interesting to note that when reruns of *Unsolved Mysteries* appeared in the USA they were shown 'almost nightly on the cable channel Lifetime – *"Television for Women"'* (Derosia, 2002: 239–40, my italics). Certainly, Fishman's research seems to concur with *Crimewatch*'s findings. While he found that on average 58.4% of the audience for his sample of reality crime programmes were female, some programmes were more popular with women than others. For example, while the audience for *Unsolved Mysteries* was more than 60% female, the audience for the more action-driven *Cops* was almost exactly equally split between men and women (Fishman, 1998: 69–70).

Surprisingly perhaps, the *Women Viewing Violence* research (Schlesinger et al., 1992) found that some women liked *Crimewatch* for being *reassuring*. This was either because they felt it demonstrated how unlikely it was that they would ever be in a position that could lead to them becoming a victim or because it showed that crime was acted on by the police and very often solved (though these women were in the minority, it must be said).[2] Fishman indicates this may again explain why *Cops* has proved less popular with female audiences than other real crime shows: 'reassurance' and intervention are sidelined, since 'It does not solicit viewer tips, and offers no pretence to catching criminals' (1998: 70). In fact *Crimewatch* strategically negotiates the challenges posed by the fact that its stories, at the time of their telling, have no closure. This is a potential problem for the programme, both in terms of fear of crime – since unsolved crimes can only mean un-convicted criminals on the streets – and in terms of providing at least some satisfactory stories for audiences generally used to the convention of closure. When the former *Crimewatch* producer Peter Chafer talked about the show 'needing results' (cited in Schlesinger and Tumber, 1995: 262) he was explicitly referring to warding off criticisms of the programme being merely exploitative, by producing tangible criminal convictions. But beyond this, the show also needs 'results' (namely endings where criminals are apprehended) to keep audiences content with its 'narratives'. Hence *Crimewatch* undertakes a variety of strategies to alleviate this and provide an ongoing and reassuring sense of resolution in ways which seek to re-inscribe a sense of classical closure; this is very often *deferred,* rather than denied.

In fact, arguably, the programme turns the problem around and uses this narrative ambiguity to its advantage with a range of updating and informing devices both within and beyond the show, helping attract a loyal audience and keep the public tuned in and feeling involved. Within the show there is constant live feedback about the kinds of calls coming in ('We just did the re-appeal on the two women suspected of fraud ... we've had a police officer call up to say that he knows one of them ... I suggest you give yourselves up now' (April 2005)) and which cases are getting good responses ('There's been a phenomenal response to the burglar rapist' (May 2000)). Together, these live updates and reminders ideally indicate that 'There really are lots of signs we might do well tonight' (June 2000). Later in the same evening of broadcast there is a 10-minute live slot, *Crimewatch Update*, purely dedicated to reminders of key clues, appeals and phone numbers, news about the calls still coming in and sometimes direct appeals to people who have called in with promising information. The programme also occasionally features follow-up interviews with families and police officers whose cases ended 'happily' and who come to the studio to express their thanks. And as noted previously, there is also a section within each show when we are briefly told the outcome of previous appeals – these resolutions are overwhelmingly positive ones, resulting in convictions, though these may have come about through independent lines of inquiry rather than through the show. Finally there are also spin-off programmes, *Crimewatch File* and *Crimewatch UK Solved*, dedicated to indepth analysis, through reconstructions and interviews, of individual cases solved with the help of *Crimewatch*. These various devices, then, provide not just a substitute sense of classical resolution for the audience but pleasure in a sense of continuity, reassurance and stability despite the episodic discourse of the programme, highlighting evidence of the programme's achievement and the ongoing value of the audience's involvement.

Further pleasure of this nature, where the programme offers the audience a kind of supportive or comforting function, can be found in the forms of address used by *Crimewatch* and its inscription, as noted in Chapter 1, of an 'invisible network' or community (Rath, 1985). The opportunity to tune in regularly and become part of this community discourse is another reassuring and pleasurable facet of the show. In its constant references to cases featured previously, the programme very much assumes an interested and regular viewer. As *Crimewatch* series producer Katie Thomson confirmed, 'We've got a big repeat audience, bigger than a lot of other programmes. People find *Crimewatch* and watch it again and again' (2002). That this sense of being *part* of the show is highly pleasurable is further endorsed by the BBC's special project audience research. The group discussions here found that 'the possibility of involvement' was a significant factor in why the programme was highly valued by most of the respondents, 'either directly (can I help?) or indirectly (I know that place)' (BBC, 1988: 2). Furthermore, when respondents described how the programme relied on help from the public a number of them did this using the terms 'we' or 'us', further demonstrating their sense of involvement. In doing so they take up the mode of address used by the presenters who, as we saw in Chapter 1, repeatedly adopt the use of 'we'.

One of the recurrent criticisms of the genre is, of course, its perceived voyeurism, earning it a reputation as 'popular peepshow entertainment' (Hebert, 1993: 6) and this kind of pleasure must also be acknowledged. Such criticisms are directed partly at reconstructions that include lascivious detail and partly at the use of CCTV footage. Certainly the access to 'forbidden' or private territory and material not always readily available in the public domain is one of the genre's enduring fascinations. Other pleasures are even more visceral. Confessing to her enjoyment of true crime in the *Guardian*, Polly Graham likens watching the genre to a fairground ride or bungee jump: 'It boils down to this; we like to feel scared' (Graham, 1994: 13). As the success of crime writers such as Patricia Cornwell, Kathy Reichs and Sara Paretsky among women readers indicates, much popular crime fiction has both a large and loyal female readership and accomplished female authors. The predominant audience for true crime literature has long been understood to be female; for example, Biressi notes that the stated target readership of *Real-Life Crimes* magazine is 68% female (2001: 3). Witness too how London's leading crime bookshop, Murder One in Charing Cross Road, is home, rather incongruously it may initially seem, not just to a massive variety of all kinds of true crime biographies, but to a huge romantic fiction collection. The apparently odd juxtaposition of books about serial killers next to Harlequin romances is perhaps less startling and more commercially rational when one notes the large numbers of women who shop there; one can even pick up flyers to join a women's crime reading group at the till. Indeed, Biressi has also noted that when new women's magazines like *Chat* and *Bella* launched in the UK in the 1980s, they adapted the traditional women's weekly into a 'tabloid package' where true crime features became a standard component of their design (2001: 5).

For Graham, true crime is more thrilling than horror films because it is 'as nitty-gritty real as you can get' (1994: 13). Here, then, there is an implication that watching true crime reconstructions on TV may serve a kind of cathartic function for women, as they confront the disturbing details of real crime in a safe, controlled and familiar environment. Indeed, series producer Katie Thomson commented that she believed *Crimewatch,*

> ... makes people feel very *empowered* against crime. We find that in two ways actually, both in the viewers and also when we interview the victims. It's the most empowering thing they can do, taking part in *Crimewatch*, in a similar way as going to trial ... being interviewed on *Crimewatch* gives them a chance to say I'm not sitting down taking this, I'm fighting back ... (2002)

From all of this we can start to envisage how *Crimewatch* viewers including, and in particular, women viewers, actually use the programme in diverse ways and gain a variety of pleasures from it. And yet, as we have seen, when the fear-of-crime panic about real crime TV took off in the 1980s, *Crimewatch* was a key player in the heated media exchanges that followed.

· FEAR OF CRIME – A FEMALE MALADY FOR MODERN TIMES? ·

I want to look more closely here, then, at how the programme featured in these deliberations, and more specifically how the debate took on gendered inflections. It was inevitable that gender would become a focus for attention in these media discussions; the second British National Crime Survey had underlined that it was *women* who were, apparently unequivocally, the most profound 'victims' of fear of crime, with 48% of women, compared to 13% of men, describing themselves as feeling 'unsafe' (Gunter, 1987: 3). Fear of crime may have been broadly invoked as a condition detrimental to society as a whole, but its actual sufferers were very much envisaged as female or feminised. Writing in *The Listener* in 1989, for example, Bob Woffinden's concerns about *Crimewatch* were typical of this mode of thought, when he observed, 'there is clearly a risk that it heightens everyday alarm, especially among the vulnerable, such as the elderly or single women' (1989: 10). These same fears and speculations had featured in the BBC's own audience research into the programme a year earlier, which had found, 'Some of the women, but none of the men, said they had been frightened by [the] programme. A few informants also mentioned the possibility of elderly viewers being frightened' (BBC, 1988: 18). What becomes clear when one examines the media coverage of the apparent rise of fear of crime, in this period and more generally, is that it is not constructed impartially as a gender-neutral condition or as concern for the general audience. Rather, it is very much conceptualised and circulated as a kind of latter-day manifestation of what Elaine Showalter has termed the 'female malady'; that is, fear of crime is represented in a manner that very much mirrors the representation of hysteria.

In her historical study of the rise of hysteria in Britain in the late nineteenth century, Showalter found,

> For centuries, hysteria had been the quintessential female malady, the very name of which derived from the Greek hysteron, or womb; but between 1870 and World War I – the 'golden age' of hysteria – it assumed a peculiarly central role in psychiatric discourse, and in definitions of femininity and female sexuality. By the end of the century, 'hysterical' had become almost interchangeable with 'feminine' in literature. (2000: 129)

Decades later, as the twentieth century drew to a close, the enduring metaphorical weight and powerful resonance of the imagery of hysteria as a means of encapsulating female irrationality, emerged again in the evocation of a host of women rendered troubled and restless by fear of crime. If we understand fear of crime to be fundamentally a condition in which the subject becomes introspective and undergoes 'ill-judged' confusion and anxiety about the real likelihood of becoming a victim, as being an 'irrational' response to external social forces and as resulting in alarming and paranoid behavioural traits, we can see how it mirrors many aspects of what Showalter identifies. Victorian society 'perceived women as childlike, irrational' (Showalter, 2000: 73); female hysterics fulfilled this cultural premise in many ways, while testing and pushing its limits to extremes, often leaving the male (i.e. 'rational') psychiatric profession frustrated and perplexed. Sufferers of fear of crime are similarly rendered apparently illogical, physically and mentally vulnerable, inherently feminised by their inability to grasp the reason and logic of 'real' crime statistics.

Understood by the psychiatric profession in the nineteenth century as a mental imbalance that led to physical symptoms such as fits, fainting, choking, sobbing and paralysis, hysteria, 'like other aspects of the feminine [seemed] elusive and enigmatic, resistant to the powers of masculine rationality' (Showalter, 2000: 129–30). In what follows, I examine how women audiences of *Crimewatch* subsequently suffer fear of crime in ways that bear remarkable structural similarities to hysteria, defying 'common sense' reason and even manifesting itself in physical responses akin to hysteria (trembling, paralysis, sleeplessness). What is also crucial to these discourses and the feminisation/representation of fear of crime among female *Crimewatch* viewers, is the place of *the home* within them. The home and television itself are a space and a medium both culturally marked as 'feminine'. Discourses about *Crimewatch* and testimonies from female viewers, particularly those watching at home alone, recurrently indicate how a powerful matrix is at work in women's reception of the programme. Given their relative rarity in comparison to, for example, either incidences of domestic violence against women or stranger attacks against men, there is undoubtedly an extremely high quota of reconstructed stranger attacks against women in the programme. This is a disparity that very much endorses the findings of Cavender et al. (1999) in relation to *America's Most Wanted*. For example, in the first three months of 2000 alone, *Crimewatch* featured four reconstructions of rape/ sexual assault cases against lone women either out or at home, two murders of lone women carried out in broad daylight and another's disappearance/suspicious death.[3] In their engagement with the programme, as outlined below, women viewers recurrently speak of their terror at seeing images and stories of other women being attacked, often in their homes. The habitual notion that the home offers a place of sanctuary to women, then, is defamiliarised in this process. This draws on a key theme of Gothic literature and film, and female Gothic in particular, where the 'hysterical' female heroine becomes overwrought and disempowered by mounting and irrational fears for her safety in an 'uncanny' home. Thus, the discourses evoking hysteria around the female viewer of *Crimewatch* very much draw on the historical association between hysteria and the Gothic sensibility.

Crucially, however, I want to argue that women's engagement with *Crimewatch* is significantly more contradictory and complex than it appears in the conventional fear-of-crime paradigm, which positions women as its 'victims'. Feminist theorists from a range of disciplines have long sought to reimagine and reclaim history's 'madwomen' in a more empowered, constructive and sympathetic light. Through interrogating the structures of a male-dominated culture that has defined and condemned women who resist patterns of conventional femininity as being 'mad', this body of work has come to see these women instead as frustrated artists, as 'failed but heroic rebels' and 'champions of a defiant womanhood' (Showalter, 2000: 4–5).[4] For Gilbert and Gubar (1984), for example, the Gothic 'madwoman in the attic' who defamiliarises the sanctity of the home destabilises and undermines the institutions of marriage and patriarchy in the process. In a similar vein, then, how too might we reimagine (the construct of) the agitated, fearful woman viewer of *Crimewatch* more productively or positively? Given the apparently debilitating effects of fear of crime and the alleged contribution of real crime TV to it, why might it be that the majority audience for *Crimewatch* is in fact women? Despite the programme's conservative hegemonic frameworks and its very real contribution to some women's fear of crime, paradoxically and simultaneously, how might women viewers also be using the programme in a productive and cathartic manner, watching it as a kind of strategy for *managing* their fear of crime? This alternative vision of the female *Crimewatch* viewer, as *using* the programme in order to explore and confront her responses to the possibility of becoming a crime victim, endows her with resilience and agency, and is thus quite at odds with the conceptualisation of the 'hysterical' female viewer as vulnerable and irrational.

· TALES OF THE GOTHIC ·

Reading descriptions given by some women of watching *Crimewatch*, one could be forgiven for thinking for a moment that one had stumbled across excerpts from a female Gothic novel. These testimonies oddly parallel images and themes that seem familiar from Victorian female 'hysterics' and madwomen, such as the narrator of Charlotte Perkins Gilman's story *The Yellow Wallpaper* (1892). In this classic Gothic tale, a woman with postpartum depression is confined under duress from her husband to take a 'rest' cure in their home, akin to solitary confinement. So distressing is this experience that she starts to imagine a shadowy figure trapped in the wallpaper of her room, and eventually descends into madness. In fact, nineteenth-century Gothic literature provides a fascinating counterpoint to the construction of women's fear of crime where again the home, which superficially represents a place of sanctuary to women, is actually revealed as a site of menace for them. Gilbert and Gubar, for example, note that literature by women in this period recurrently '[uses] houses as primary symbols of female imprisonment' (1984: 85). Reason gives way to 'irrational' fears as the heroine begins to suspect she is being stalked by a malign presence in one form or another and her very sanity seems under threat. Similarly, in fear of crime testimonies, women frequently speak of their terror at the prospect of stranger attacks in the home, though statistically this kind of crime is extremely rare.

Of course, women have long been encouraged by patriarchal culture to view the 'outside' world as a place that leaves them vulnerable, a place where they should seek to be escorted and chaperoned, thus enabling patriarchy to police their sex(uality).[5] There is, of course, a contradiction inherent in this that patriarchal culture struggles to contain; that is, that women are in fact at greater risk of violence and abuse *within* the private sphere of the home. Fred Botting describes the significance of the home to nineteenth-century Gothic in the following way:

> As the privileged site of Victorian culture, home and family were seen as the last refuge from the sense of loss and the forces threatening social relations. The home however, could be a prison as well as a refuge ... the home is the site of both internal and external pressures, uncanny and terrifying at the same time. (1996: 128)

In *Crimewatch*, the 'external pressure' of stranger attacks emanating from the outside world infiltrates the 'internal' space of the home, to the extent that it deflects attention away from the far more real threat of attacks against women from their intimates and familiars. Women discussing the programme recurrently describe how, after watching it, preoccupied by the fear of an intruder, they fear to venture alone around their homes and do not feel safe there. For example, consider this account from one of the respondents in the *Women Viewing Violence* research discussing *Crimewatch*:

> When I have watched it in the past, it's made me nervous, like when I've had to go upstairs thinking 'God I'm not safe', because they have shown a lot of scenes where things have happened within your own home. When people have come when you could be in bed and that ... (Schlesinger et al., 1992: 51)

One sees here exactly how the act of watching TV at home, and in so doing seeing other women being attacked in their homes, becomes an acutely disturbing experience that defamiliarises the female viewer's own home. In a similar vein, the following account from Polly Graham writing in the *Guardian*, reads like a scene straight from a slasher movie:

> Babysitting for friends in a creaking Victorian house, I mistakenly watched *Crimewatch*. For the rest of the night I huddled motionless on the sofa, flinching at every noise. It got darker, but I couldn't draw the curtains for fear of the phantom in the shrubbery. I sat like this until my friends came home. (1994: 13)

Though one suspects a note of irony here, the image evoked is nevertheless a familiar stereotype of excessive female paranoia and gothic foreboding where again the home is made 'uncanny'. Likewise, Jean Ross confesses that her neurosis is such that for her 'thrillers are out, as are programmes such as *Crimewatch*' since she is the self-diagnosed victim of an 'over-voracious imagination'. Her home too transforms at night from domestic haven to site of terror:

> But what was that? I sit bolt upright in bed. I surely heard a door opening? I slide noiselessly out of bed and tiptoe across the landing, my heart pounding, my ears straining for further evidence of intrusion. I sit on the top step of the stairs and resume my lonely vigil. It is 4am and I am home alone. By day I am an eminently sensible woman. But turn the clock round to midnight, remove my husband to foreign climes and you will see before you a neurotic wreck, whose nerves explode at the slightest creak of a central heating pipe. (J. Ross, 1992: 19)

What these 'hysterical' responses repeatedly indicate, as the Gothic genre characteristically suggests, is that there is no space, public or private, clearly defined as safe for women.[6] Other respondents in Schlesinger et al.'s audience research again bear out how pervasive this sensibility is among the 'nervous' *Crimewatch* female audience. For example, one comments,

> I think [*Crimewatch*] still frightens you, really. But I do watch it. I mean my husband's on nights when I watched it this week ... and my alarm is on. That's the only thing that reassures me, I've got real brilliant alarms in the house. That's the only way I feel safe in my house. (Schlesinger et al., 1992: 69–70)

Like the female hysteric, these women evidence physical responses brought on by mental anxiety, speaking of insomnia and pounding hearts, of 'huddling motionless' and 'flinching'. Interestingly too, as Ellen Moers notes, it was precisely the intention of Gothic literature to produce physiological responses to fear, 'to get to the body itself' (1986: 90), a sensation that the crime appeal format seems to replicate entirely here. In another particularly emotive and moving testimony drawn from the BBC's audience research, one woman describes her specific distress at a reconstruction where 'two little old ladies' were attacked in their remote country house; 'When you saw them, to think that someone could do that to them. You start cracking. It makes me cry' (BBC, 1988: 18a). This melancholic image of 'cracking', of the body literally giving up under the stress wrought by the programme and fear of crime, is a painfully striking one that powerfully encapsulates the potential harm such stories may well hold for some audience members.

· HYSTERICAL TELEVISION ·

To understand women's responses to *Crimewatch* more fully, however, we need more than statistics and testimony; we must look too at the text itself and recognise *Crimewatch*'s resonance within the medium and institution of British television, particularly for women audiences. As we have seen, television, according to many critics including Ellis (1994) and Auslander (1999), is a medium characterised by its qualities of intimacy and familiarity. It is quintessentially a *domestic* object and by extension, then, is pervasively characterised as a feminised object in many ways. While the 'technology' surrounding TV may (traditionally at least) have been conceptualised as 'male' (Gray, 1987), its 'consumption' has been predominantly 'female'. Ellis argues that TV conceptualises its audience as 'the family' (1994: 113)[7] but the notion of the family itself is one that is inextricably grounded in the feminine. *Crimewatch* undeniably holds a powerful place in its female audience's experience of crime and television, as evidenced by the women's responses described above, and indeed in comments made by *Crimewatch*'s producers during my interviews with them. Assistant producer Belinda Phillips, for example, described how, 'I spoke to a woman last year, when I was answering the phones, and she said she'd watched every single *Crimewatch* since 1984'. On another occasion, 'A policewoman on the programme said she'd watched since she was a little girl and that's what inspired her to join the police' (Phillips, 2002).

Of course, all these examples and testimonies from women about their investment in the programme are isolated instances, anecdotes if you like, not 'empirical' research. But a more comprehensive understanding of the nature of audience engagement with television arguably lies precisely in uncovering the anecdotal and deeming it 'worthy' of academic attention, since much of our experience of television takes place precisely in these conversational exchanges. Indeed, in a methodological parallel that crosses inter-disciplinary boundaries, John Tulloch too has endorsed 'a qualitative approach to the "micro-narratives" of "lay-knowledge"' in his work on fear of crime (2000: 186). None of these stories 'prove' anything in isolation; together, with all the other 'evidence' garnered from press reports, producers' accounts and existing audience research, they build a picture that indicates just how potent *Crimewatch* is in British women's experience of fear of crime, crime and television. It is, after all, no exaggeration to call it the longest-running and best-known 'crime series' on contemporary British television. *Crimewatch*'s representation of female victims of crime, then, carries the burden of a huge cultural resonance for many members of its female audience, which makes its capacity for sensationalism in some reconstructions all the more potentially problematic. When the prevalence and habitual explicitness of attacks against women seen in the programme is acknowledged, women's responses to it start to seem rather less 'neurotic'.

For example, a February 2000 appeal asked for help to identify a leather fetishist attacker who had broken into women's homes, viciously assaulted them in some instances and demanded they produce their leather purses or gloves. The reconstruction opens with a woman at home alone watching television one evening, thus exactly mirroring the female viewer who may be home alone herself watching *Crimewatch*. We can actually see she is watching the popular BBC1 soap *EastEnders*, underlining the scene's authenticity; *Crimewatch* viewers may have been watching primetime soaps themselves earlier that very evening. When she answers an apparently innocent knock at the door, her attacker bursts in with a bag on his head. A quite explicitly violent scene ensues where we see him grab the woman by the throat, place a hand over her mouth and drag her inside as she shrieks and struggles in blind panic. In a few short seconds, then, we see the precariousness of the sanctity of the home and women's safety there. An initially everyday scene, which the lone female viewer will be replicating at home as she watches *Crimewatch*, becomes a nightmare. She watches her onscreen surrogate endure the horror that haunts her.

Similarly, in the June 2000 edition, the reconstruction of a series of sex attacks in Chichester features some prolonged interior shots of the rapist with his victims, having broken into their bedrooms. On two occasions during this reconstruction we see the intruder in the act of stirring women as they lie sleeping and blissfully unaware of his presence in their darkened bedrooms, standing over them and waking them with a hand over their mouth, tying them up and threatening them. One of the victims, a student, tells in voiceover how it was an ordinary night where she got ready for bed in the normal way, making a cup of tea, putting her music on and getting into bed, everyday images that are reconstructed in a naturalistic way. She goes on to say that the thing that most sticks in her mind and still 'freaks her out' was waking up to find him standing there, a scene we now witness.

Now, however, her bedroom has changed. The bedroom is quite literally transformed during the course of the reconstruction once the intruder infiltrates it. Gone is the naturalistic setting of a moment ago. Instead her bedroom is dramatically swathed in blue light. Why the aesthetic shift? These scenes, marked by suspense with their tense pacing and dramatic build-up and lit in shadowy and evocative blue tones, recall images from Hollywood thrillers, the territory of *Jagged Edge* (US, dir. Marquand, 1985) or *Manhunter* (US, dir. Mann, 1986) rather than an attempt at factual reporting. The same victim explains, 'I was absolutely petrified. My heart was beating really hard and really fast. From then on I thought I was dead, I really did', as we see her terrified face and the rapist binding her hands together, telling her not to scream in a lengthy and disturbing exchange, the details of which might very easily have been paraphrased in the commentary. We also hear the brave and inspirational testimony of a rape survivor when she says, 'He's really picked the wrong girl 'cos I'm such a strong person'. But what is predominantly dwelt on, and what is likely to remain most evocative in the viewer's recall of this reconstruction, is its structure and images, the building of anticipation, tension, horror and suspense as we witness the attacker's movements in his victim's bedrooms; images that, as the women viewers' testimonies above describe, are particularly potent in women's fear of crime.

In June 2005 (a programme that features a serial sex attacker in Cambridgeshire, the murder of a woman prostitute in Glasgow and the attempted rape of a woman in London) we see again how enduringly pervasive this kind of reconstruction is. In the hunt for a serial sex offender in St Neots, Ross introduces the reconstruction by telling us, 'Cambridge police have linked as many as 10 offences and there may be many, many others, each more serious than the last'. We open on a particularly ominous note then; what is frightening here is the seemingly endless capacity for this man to offend, the unknowability of the extent of his attacks ('there may be many, many others'). The reconstruction starts with a fast-paced montage of different women screaming, crying, stripping off in front of a masked assailant over a soundtrack of haunting music, as Bruce's introductory voiceover tells us, 'Police believe one man is responsible for an escalating series of sex offences ... '. The reconstruction then features three of the attacks-first, a woman is followed home in the early hours and pushed inside her house as she opens the front door. In a terrifying exchange her attacker screams at her to get her trousers off as she tries to fight him and he finally runs away when her phone rings. In the next attack, the assailant breaks into a woman's home after watching her husband leave for work. As she sleeps upstairs, oblivious to what is happening, the programme adopts the standard classical suspense technique by cross-cutting between images of her in bed and his feet creeping up the stairs. Then his masked face leers into the camera, positioning us as the victim waking up to find him above her, and another hysterical, horrifying fight ensues.

In the final attack, a woman is sleeping at home with her young daughter in bed beside her. We see a man peeping through the window looking at her, before she realises someone is in the house. Indeed, recognising the terrifying yet oddly familiar nature of what is happening and pre-empting the aesthetics of the way these images will be reconstructed, she comments in the voiceover, 'It was like something out of a horror film'. When he breaks into the room screaming at her to take her top off, the camera (i.e. 'we', the viewer) is positioned low, as if in bed (like the victim). He runs directly at the camera as he comes screaming into the room, screaming at *us*, as we are positioned again with the victim's point of view. In another distressing scene we see the victim forced to strip, hear how she feared for her daughter's life and finally see her distract him and climb naked out of the window to escape. How much of what we see here had to be reconstructed? How much of it might have been summarised in voiceover? And, of course, there is no question raised regarding why it took so long for the cases to be linked. Both Belinda Phillips and Katie Thomson at *Crimewatch* were keen to stress the programme's sensitivity regarding the representation of women and violent crime. Phillips commented that, 'The golden rule is don't show anything that isn't necessary. We just want to show what's necessary. We don't want to show people being frightened' (2002). But analysis of these reconstructions reveals that, like the advice laid out in the BBC's *Producers' Guidelines*, the interpretation of what is 'necessary' is a hugely subjective matter.

Like the Gothic genre, then, these tales transform the home. They reveal the contradiction of 'the home' for women; a place that is conventionally meant to be marked as a secure space for the feminine is exposed as fraught and dangerous. But Gothic literature has been re-appropriated by feminist criticism as ideologically transgressive precisely because it defamiliarises the home, often in part by pointing the finger at the heroine's intimates or male authorities as the source of her intimidation. In Kilgour's words,

> The female gothic itself is not a ratification but an exposé of domesticity and the family, through the technique of estrangement or romantic defamiliarisation: by cloaking familiar images of domesticity in gothic forms, it enables us to see that the home is a prison, in which the helpless female is at the mercy of ominous patriarchal authorities. (1995: 9)

It thereby 'exposes' conventional domesticity as repressive towards women, even if this ideology is apparently or superficially recuperated by the (unsatisfactory) resolution of the 'happy ending' (Kilgour, 1995: 8–9). By comparison, however, while *Crimewatch*'s reconstructions may lead women to question the evidently unstable social construct of the home as their haven, these narratives remain socially repressive for suggesting that even in their own homes, it is *strangers* who women must fear, not the intimates who are in reality the greatest threat to them.

For the female viewer of *Crimewatch*, like the Gothic heroine, the line between 'real' and 'imagined' threat is not a straightforward or distinct one, but this is in no sense to belittle her fears. Rather, we must revisit where such anxieties spring from and why it is considered a 'feminine' trait to hold them. The notion that women are particularly given to over-active imaginations is an enduring facet of the gendered stereotyping of women, embedded in both the Gothic genre and the construction of the female victim of fear of crime, again helping sustain the depiction of them as childlike and irrational. For example, the BBC's women *Crimewatch* viewers discussed how when watching alone, 'You're [sic] imagination starts taking over' – 'Particularly at night when you're getting tired as well' (BBC, 1988: 18a). However, the Gothic heroine is typically vindicated by the revelation that there really was a menacing party threatening her in some sense. For the nervous female viewer of *Crimewatch* too, their sense of menace is also linked to valid concerns and a genuine, albeit statistically unlikely, threat, rather than merely being the by-product of an 'over-voracious' imagination such as Jean Ross confesses to above (1992: 19). Yet the discourses surrounding these 'vulnerable' women frequently invite us to see their responses as enduringly paranoid, rather than a legitimate reaction to actual social issues and conditions.

There is an internal paradox in the programme whereby it recurrently reminds women they are under threat from stranger-attacks both in the streets and in the home – then tells them, in presenter Nick Ross's signature sign-off, 'Don't have nightmares. Do sleep well'. This obscures the fact that it is domestic violence that women are most likely to experience, the threat of which is, of course, most pronounced in the home, an issue almost never touched on by the programme.[8] Indeed this issue is further obscured by the fact that, again like the female Gothic's ultimate (apparent) endorsement of romance, the fear of crime discourse also finally operates as a means of normalising, promoting and condoning women's incorporation into conventional, heterosexual relationships. Again, this reinforces what we saw in Chapter 3, that the programme endorses the normalcy and desirability of 'the family' as a means of legitimising its victims. This deflects attention away from the fact that for many female victims of violence it is precisely 'the family' that is the source of their 'victimisation'.

The vision of heterosexuality implicit in fear-of-crime commentaries very much inscribes men as protectors of women, as alleviators of women's paranoia about crime and lone women as defenceless women. Woffinden, as we saw above, is particularly concerned about the vulnerability of *'single* women' (1989: 10). Women too are co-opted into this viewpoint; in addition to the women in Schlesinger et al.'s research who speak fearfully of watching the programme alone ('It does heighten your perception of everything, I think – if you are *on your own*' (1992: 70)); Jean Ross is particularly vulnerable when her husband is away and she is 'home *alone*' (1992: 19, my italics); Graham is too scared to move till her 'friends come home' (1994: 13); while the BBC's women respondents speculate, 'I think if I was on my own I wouldn't watch it' – 'It might make people a bit nervous if on their own' (BBC, 1988: 18). The implication is that if you're a woman, you will be/feel safer in the care of a man, thus encouraging women to seek solace and security in the conventional social spaces of families and heterosexual relationships. Indeed, Sandra Walklate has criticised the way fear-of-crime surveys have tended to ask questions that 'focus on when the individual is alone, reflecting an assumption that this is the behavioural condition in which fear is most likely to be experienced' (1995: 58). This maintains a misleading distinction that particularly obscures a more expansive acknowledgement of women's experience of crime and the ubiquity of violence *within* the home.

· REIMAGINING FEAR OF CRIME ·

However, the image of fear of crime as a debilitating female condition belies many things. In fact, many of the assumptions that form the foundations of our conceptualisation of 'fear of crime' are questionable, as is the image of women as 'victims' of fear of crime. First, if fear of crime incurs an 'irrational' response to the actual likelihood of crime occurring, then we must ask how 'irrationality' is defined. In Walklate's words, 'Whose standards are being used as the markers of a reasonable or a rational fear? Whose standards are being used as a marker of connecting that reasonable or rational fear to risk?' (1995: 68). Not, presumably, women's. Indeed for Walklate, these questions are implicated in the 'masculinist interpretation and debate' that has informed much of criminology's work in this arena, where gendered definitions of 'irrational' fears, 'risk' and 'dangerous behaviour' are interwoven. In her words, 'This particular way of understanding risk, tied as it is to particular views of what counts as rational knowledge and who can possess such knowledge, is a fundamental reflection of criminology's inability to see how its own conceptual schema is a gendered one' (Walklate, 1995: 76).

In contrast to the implicit denigration of women's appraisal of risk seen in much fear of crime research, feminist criminology has argued that women's knowledge must be treated as 'expert knowledge', recognising how they are best placed to comment on 'the routinised, daily threat to personal security which characterises many women's lives' (Walklate, 1995: 67). On a similar note elsewhere, Tulloch has called for a more expansive conceptualisation and acknowledgement of women's everyday experience of crime that would acknowledge how women's daily lives must negotiate a 'whole spectrum of cues to fear – the man across the carriage staring fixedly at you, the man in the seat next to you whose knee nestles into yours each time the train lurches' (2000: 187). Men simply do not experience the same spectrum; if definitions drawn from their experience are predominantly adopted in order to delineate what constitutes 'rational' fear, then of course, by default, women's might appear 'irrational'.

Second, the vision of female irrationality implicit in fear-of-crime debates belies the fact that women are constantly bombarded with (often conflicting) information about their vulnerability, in the light of which their fear of crime becomes far from unreasonable (Soothill and Walby, 1991). For example, the day after the BBC announced its new crime reporting guidelines in June 1994, in an attempt to reassure the public that their fear of crime was unwarranted, Polly Toynbee wrote in the *Guardian* that, 'Most attacks are domestic, men attacking their lovers and wives. Yet women and old people live in growing irrational fear of attack by a stranger on the street' (1994: 20). Toynbee's words here seemingly endorse a number of worrying assumptions. First, by seeking to 'reassure' women that most attacks are domestic it almost transforms domestic violence into a lesser crime. Second, she demonstrates again my argument that the fear of crime is perceived as a problem for certain 'vulnerable' groups, namely women and the elderly, the implication being that men have a better grip on reality and are somehow able to rationalise the statistics and media reports in a more reasonable and astute fashion. Third, even though she herself goes on to criticise the way media and politicians represent crime, these fears are trivialised as 'irrational'.

But the 'facts', when we see them, about the improbability of women suffering stranger attack lie in stark contrast to the coverage of such assaults that *saturate* the media's representation of fictional and real life accounts of crime. It is this phenomenon that begins to account for the way in which the fear of crime is marked predominantly as a female malady. *Crimewatch's* preoccupation with stranger assaults on women is difficult to reconcile with the programme's own reminders that women's fears 'for the vast majority are unwarranted' and 'attacks by strangers very rare' (March 2000). In fact, one of the respondents in Schlesinger et al. tackles the programme's inconsistent position on this matter, and the sensationalism of the media more generally, when she points to the excessive coverage of these 'rare' crimes; 'I didn't like the bit where she says the cases are rarer than – what? Because it's not really [true]. Because you lift the papers, you get it in the papers day in and day out. You get it on the telly day in and day out' (1992: 69). The debate among these women respondents, who also critiqued the reconstruction of the murder of a young woman hitch-hiker for focusing on the victim rather than the assailant, suggests a level of critical consciousness among women that the 'irrationality' of women's fear of crime doesn't generally credit them with.

· WOMEN 'USING' *CRIMEWATCH* ·

Finally, then, we need not necessarily understand these nervous female *Crimewatch* viewers as being *victims* of fear of crime. Rather we might also understand them as women *managing* their fear of crime. Watching real crime reconstructions on TV may in fact have a kind of cathartic function for women, as they confront the disturbing details of real crime in a safe, controlled and familiar environment. Cavender et al. (1999) have critiqued (unpublished) work by Deborah Barber about *Crimewatch*'s US counterpart, *America's Most Wanted,* in which she argued that 'the program empowers women to speak about their victimisation' (Cavender et al., 1999: 643). They conclude that Barber's premise is unpersuasive since the programme '(re) creates a portrait of peril and disseminates subordinating images of women' (Cavender et al., 1999: 659). While my research very much confirms their findings in terms of uncovering the same broadly ideologically conservative structures present in *Crimewatch*, this is not to say that some women may not use the programme to the kinds of 'empowering' ends Barber alludes to and which *Crimewatch* producer Katie Thomson described above. This would be to delimit the possibilities of its reception, to elevate the text to a kind of omniscience, privileging it above the audience as the pre-eminent site of meaning-making.

Rather, women's evident fascination for real crime and their place as the majority audience of both *Crimewatch* and *America's Most Wanted* (Fishman, 1998: 70) may indeed suggest that they reap some kind of empowerment from the texts, in spite of the genre's hegemonic frameworks. Arguably *Crimewatch* allows them to engage with, explore and confront fear of crime in a controlled environment, even though its representations of crime are clearly heavily mediated. Though perhaps less immediately pragmatic in its application, such a conceptualisation is akin to the strategies Tulloch uncovered among women in his Australian fear of crime research project. Discussing their nervousness about using public transport in Sydney, his female respondents spoke, for example, of sitting in particular spots on the train home at night or carrying an apple in order to legitimise carrying a knife, strategies Tulloch refers to as 'adaptive coping' (2000: 186–7). Watching *Crimewatch* too, then, may be a form of 'adaptive coping' for women in a culture where they are continually reminded of their vulnerability.

For example, Polly Graham's commentary on watching 'real life crime programmes' in 1994 discusses the generic traits of the form. She talks somewhat mockingly about the very formulaic nature of the genre's reconstructions, presentational style and police interviews which make the playing out of terrible crimes, despite their inherent irresolution and mystery, rather predictable:

> These programmes are as formulaic as Mills and Boon. First the reconstruction of the crime – the practised voice-over reminds us that 'actors play the main parts' while the reconstruction shows how easily everyday life is turned upside down. Next they wheel on the camera-shy officer in charge with the all important and usually quite comical description of the attacker ... And so it goes on. (Graham, 1994: 13)

Arguably this formulaic quality brings with it a sense of familiarity; in this way real crime operates in a standard generic fashion and, like any other genre, follows patterns and rewards knowledge of these traits by endowing the audience with a sense of expertise. The nature of this relationship again lends support to my proposition that true crime reconstructions allow women to consolidate their attitudes to crime in a safe environment. The formulaic nature of *Crimewatch* even allows Graham to imagine herself in the place of the victim. She goes on to describe how, 'Sometimes, walking home alone at night I imagine a reconstruction of my own murder. The echoes of my footsteps fade-out as *Crimewatch*'s Nick Ross says: "Two days later her body was found by a woman walking her dog"' (Graham, 1994: 13).

Graham observes 'This is not healthy behaviour' and it may indeed seem a rather morbid reverie that apparently demonstrates the paranoia that fear of crime gives rise to. But it is also a fascinating reflection on Graham's engagement with the show. Her imagined reconstruction is very much a formulaic 'woman's' murder; she is alone, it is night, her footsteps echo, something too horrible to contemplate happens, her dead body is concealed.

This account, then, is more than the vivid imagination of a woman consumed by fear of crime. It is far more telling, in that it points to a possibly ironic and/or cathartic mechanism for dealing with accounts of other women's murders and the potential to become a victim herself; she plays out this fear in self-conscious fashion like a spectator watching a Hollywood movie. This is a startling example of the complex and contradictory engagement the woman viewer may have with *Crimewatch,* a problematical relationship that I would argue is quite common. She simultaneously acknowledges the programme's contribution to her fear of crime and critiques it, in this instance undermining its potency by parodying it, foregrounding her awareness of its staple formulaic images and narratives. Though this does not excuse the programme's tendency for sensationalism nor underestimate the potentially serious ramifications of this for some women, the woman viewer whose fear of crime is, by her own admission, enhanced by *Crimewatch* is not necessarily a 'cultural dupe'.

Showalter describes how the Victorian hysterics proved a particularly unpopular and irksome breed among the male psychiatric profession, 'disagreeable and disliked' for their uncooperative ways (2000: 134). Again, we should remember Showalter's caution that we recognise the desperation of these women and not romanticise them, nor endorse their actions as laudable. But it is nevertheless strangely gratifying to think of them leaving their medics, figureheads of a patriarchal culture that systematically repressed and constrained women, so apparently vexed. Within these constraints, by making themselves 'a problem' they demanded and won attention in a culture that steadfastly marginalised them; their 'irrational' behaviour at the very least made its roots a topic of some debate; they made women's rage visible even while its causes remained unspoken or suppressed. In doing so, despite their ultimate powerlessness, they became 'powerful antagonists' (Showalter, 2000: 133). For these reasons too, female 'victims' of fear of crime are their sisters; while the full nature of women's engagement with the threat of violent crime and the role of television within that is still far from being properly understood or addressed, these women have also, at the very least, made these issues a necessary and significant part of our cultural agendas. When we consider the conflictual, sensationalistic and misleading nature of the media's representation of crime against women, when we reimagine the female viewer of *Crimewatch* or *America's Most Wanted* as *using* the programmes in order to confront and explore her fear of crime, the notion of the hysterical female viewer loses its currency. Rather, the true source of hysteria in all of this – thriving on emotional outbursts, trading in frenzy and anxiety – is arguably the media itself.

· NOTES ·

1 Elsewhere, in the US Cavender and Bond-Maupin found in their analysis of *America's Most Wanted* and *Unsolved Mysteries* that only 4% of their sample 'vignettes' featured female criminals, and then as 'accomplices' (1993: 308).

2 Schlesinger et al., 1992: 55–70. Significantly this response revealed the importance of cultural difference, since Asian women were those most likely to say that the programme decreased their fear of crime. This was attributed to the fact that cultural restrictions on their freedom of movement decreased their likelihood of being attacked by strangers. What this finding also points to again, however, is how commonly the threat of violence within the home is subordinated to fear of stranger attacks, despite the former being more likely.

3 Of course, this is not to suggest that we should understand 'women' as constituting a homogeneous group, be that as an audience for the programme or as victims represented within it. Class, age, sexuality and race all undoubtedly play a part in the way *Crimewatch* constructs its female victims and in the way different women experience fear of crime, but space here prohibits me from examining the role of these additional elements of identity formation in greater detail.

4 As Showalter warns, however, this kind of approach can run the risk of 'endorsing madness as a desirable form of rebellion rather than seeing it as the desperate communication of the powerless' (2000: 5). Thus feminist criticism of this kind must be cautious not to romanticise 'madness' in its quest to vindicate these women.

5 *Crimewatch* endorses this premise too, even while representing women as vulnerable in the *home*; hence C. Kay Weaver, in an essay entitled '*Crimewatch UK* – Keeping Women off the Streets', argues that 'crime reconstructions help promote the power of a gendered hegemony by reinforcing women's fears for their safety in public spaces' (1998: 248).

6 Again this mirrors the conclusions of Cavender et al. in the US, who found that whatever measures they adopted to circumvent crime, 'The world is a dangerous place for women on *America's Most Wanted*' (1999: 660).

7 More broadly, this notion is increasingly under threat in the modern multi-channel, multi-set household.

8 I use the term 'domestic violence' advisedly since, as Cynthia Carter has pointed out, this is an expression that can seem to distinguish unhelpfully between the sorts of violence women suffer within and outside the home and imply that domestic violence isn't rooted in sexual violence (C. Carter, 1998a: 8). Nevertheless it is still a resonant term here since it is precisely, as the term suggests, violence against women *within the home* that is absent in *Crimewatch* and this connotation is one which is still implied, and distinctive, in the popular usage of the term. Of course, as an appeal programme predominantly seeking to identify unidentified criminal suspects and perpetrators, domestic violence is arguably inappropriate to *Crimewatch*'s remit; but nevertheless its absence contributes to the media's commonplace misrepresentation of the kinds of crime women are most likely to suffer.

Conclusion

NEGOTIATING BOUNDARIES IN REAL CRIME AND REALITY TV

Writing about the rise of 'reality TV' in 1994, a genre he takes to include programmes ranging from *Cops* to *America's Most Wanted*, to *Rescue 911,* Bill Nichols has observed,

> Any firm sense of boundary which such shows attempt to uphold between fact and fiction, narrative and exposition, storytelling and reporting inevitably blurs ... Everything is up for grabs in a gigantic reshuffling of the stuff of everyday life. Everything, that is, is subject to interpretation by television as a story-telling machine. (1994: 43)

It is this constant return to the problem of 'blurring' in both academic and journalistic discourses that seems to me to be precisely the term most pointedly at stake throughout the debates that real crime TV has figured in. Biressi and Nunn, for example, note how 'new reality genres of crime and emergency services programming' since the 1990s 'blur the boundaries between the public and private sphere, amalgamating the primary aims to inform and entertain in to one unique package' (2005: 120–1). Elsewhere, Fishman and Cavender seem to sound a note of familiar disapproval when they observe, 'Television reality programs are especially hard to categorise because they blur the line between news and entertainment: some even blur the line between fact and fiction' (1998: 3). This anxiety about 'reshuffling' can focus on the blurring of fact and fiction, the blurring of entertainment with information, the blurring of police/public/journalistic roles or the blurring of public service television's 'responsibilities' with the drive to boost ratings. Whichever form it takes, the interest in the 'collapse' of such distinctions, as Nichols's rather apocalyptic description above suggests, is testimony both to the power this blurring holds in our imaginations and to the fears it suggests about the future and quality of television – and arguably British television in particular. As we settle into the twenty-first century and as the ubiquity of real crime TV and reality TV generally shows no signs of abating, this seems an appropriate juncture to ask whether these binaries can continue to hold any water in the contemporary televisual landscape. Rather than expressing fears about television's alleged 'blurring' of boundaries, has the time come instead to look at how television *negotiates boundaries*'?

In fact, the 'nervousness' surrounding television's propensity for blurring genre boundaries and manipulating 'the real' in particular has something of a tradition in critical debates surrounding the medium (see Roscoe and Hight, 2001). This can be related to a long history of fears both for and about the television audience, who, it is implied, might be unable to engage critically with 'hybrid' or otherwise complex forms. Such fears are bound up in issues of class and cultural value, and are arguably characterised by a paternalistic and conservative impulse that, within the terms of the mass-culture tradition, constructs the mass-audience as vulnerable and malleable. The reception of early 'real crime' programming emerging in the mid-1980s provides a good illustration of such discourses. For example, writing in *The Listener* about the emergence of *Crimewatch* in Britain in 1984, Benjamin Woolley commented, 'The problem with reconstructions is that they are presented as being indistinguishable from real events and this confuses at least a few members of the audience' (1984: 10). This kind of critique in no way recognises how *Crimewatch*'s reconstructions are very often quite anti-realist or even surreal in their rendering; such inventiveness or creative licence is sometimes needed in order to try and make sense of these incomplete stories and their ellipses. By necessity there is always a movement between 'fact' and (informed) speculation in the reconstructions, sometimes leading to negotiation or slippage between different narrative traditions and conventions, from the use of real forensic evidence to surreal and abstract imagery.

Witness, for example, how the moment when robbers broke into a jewellers in Stratford-upon-Avon (tx 13 April 2005) is shown three times in quick succession in three slightly altered ways, in order to illustrate three different witness perspectives; how in April 2000, in the reconstruction of Jill Dando's murder, a large disembodied question mark floats on to the screen over the image of the mysterious man seen lurking in her road; how the suspicious death of art student Jessie Earl features not merely the pragmatic business of clues and evidence, but excerpts read from her diary, and scenes of seagulls reeling in the sky, as a woman's voice describes a trip to the cliffs where she walked with her 'arms spread out like sails' (tx February 2000). It seems unlikely that any of these scenes could be thought of as 'indistinguishable from real events'.[1] Five years after Woolley was writing, similar kinds of anxieties were at stake in Bob Woffinden's observation that, 'Clearly the public has a voracious appetite for true-life crime. And *Crimewatch* has enhanced entertainment value; quite simply it's better because it's real. A kind of blurring of distinctions thus occurs' (Woffinden, 1989: 10). But as Kilborn notes, 'it is important to distinguish between actual and presumed audience responses … viewers are far more critically aware than they are often given credit for, thus belying some of the more gloomy prognostications of the cultural pessimists' (2003: 15).

Looked at another way, the generic fluidity that has made some commentators so nervous about the reception of real crime TV and its use of reconstructions might equally be said to be evident in *news* coverage. Nichols has gone as far as to point out 'the proximity of news to circus', arguing, as numerous other commentators have, that its entertainment function is evident in the way it 'borrows' from the characteristics of 'fiction'. For example,

> Network news makes heavy use of melodramatic codings in its representations of reality. It recounts events as tales between forces of good and evil, between 'our' family and 'theirs' in foreign news, and as a tale of conflict, rivalry, sacrifice, or betrayal among members of our own family in domestic news. (Nichols, 1994: 49–50)

One cannot help but conclude, then, that such 'blurring' is less a cause for media concern when it occurs in news, since the audience for news is constructed as, or assumed to be, educated and rational and thus able to cope with generic reconfiguring. By contrast the rather less distinct, less 'known' and therefore more culturally perturbing audience for real crime programmes needs paternalistic 'protection' from the confusion and even harm that such ambiguity might apparently lead to. These fears become all the more potent and loaded when one recalls that *Crimewatch* and other real crime programmes have been found to have a predominantly female and/or working- to lower-middle-class audience; something disapproving critiques of the programme have very often seemed to suspect. Katie Thomson from *Crimewatch* confirmed that their audience research had indicated they have slightly more female viewers and 'quite a low demograph in that it's more C/D than A/B' (2002). Meanwhile in the US, the Fox network consciously developed *America's Most Wanted* to target the low-income audience neglected by the three major networks, apparently with some success, while on average it achieves an audience which is nearly 60% female (Fishman, 1998: 66–9). To what extent, then, might fears of the crime appeal programme's generic 'blurring' really amount to fears of its audience?

In fact, the 'blurring' of boundaries described above and the difficulty of ascribing a definition to the reconstruction form(s) was contentious long before the explosion of real crime programming in the 1980s; the terms 'faction', 'drama-documentary' and 'reconstruction' have all historically involved attempts to find a truly embracing way of describing what this 'form', in these different inflections, does. Though there are many shades of grey encompassed within the terms 'reconstruction' and 'drama-doc' and they should not merely be conflated, its mix of 'fact' (real crimes and victims) and 'fiction' (actors playing these out) is one of the reasons that *Crimewatch* and its crime appeal compatriots have been controversial around the world, as if this mixing of traits is disingenuous or unethical in some way. Indeed, until recently at least, drama-documentary has perhaps been the most controversial form in the history of British television, as the massive debates that met the work of drama-documentarists such as Peter Watkins (*The War Game*, 1966), Ken Loach and Tony Garnett (*Cathy Come Home*, 1966) evidenced. *The War Game,* for example, was initially banned by the BBC for its perceived disingenuity, a 'documentary' about a nuclear attack in Britain, which it was feared would cause confusion and panic among audiences who would take it as 'the real thing'. Yet the debates evoked by drama-documentary might be traced back further still to John Grierson's famous and rather equivocal description of documentary as *'the creative interpretation of reality'*, (cited in Kerr, 1990: 77, my italics) highlighting as far back as the 1930s that there have never been any easy distinctions between 'drama' and 'reality'.

Now, in the twenty-first century, discourses that admonish the breakdown of traditional generic boundaries and the manipulation of 'the real' continue to haunt reality TV. It appears that cultural critics and academics very often remain reluctant to relinquish evidently inadequate binaries, even while shifts in television programming increasingly demand that we must. This isn't to say that the distinctions of 'fact' and 'fiction' have absolutely no meaning in themselves at all any more; but rather that (as reality TV clearly demonstrates), since these terms are always under 'construction' and 'negotiation', our definitions of the relationship between television and realism, 'fact' and 'fiction' and 'factual' and 'entertainment' shows must also adapt. Yet the preoccupation with the (it is often implied somehow deceitful) capacity of television to 'blur boundaries' continues, deflecting attention away from seeking out new conceptualisations and methodological approaches that might move debates forward. Thus one of the most striking features of the popular and critical reception of reality TV has been comment on the ways in which it manipulates and constructs 'the real' and hence the contested nature of the term 'reality TV' itself ('the two words are mutually exclusive' (Clark, 2002: 6)). Audiences, critics, academics and actual participants in reality TV, have become engaged across popular culture in discussion of the form's play with editing, characterisation, dramatic structures, aesthetics and their effects, in an entirely self-reflexive fashion. In fact, Corner (2001) identifies 'new levels of representational play and reflexivity' as a defining feature of 'popular factual entertainment' or 'documentary as diversion'. As reality TV formats have continued to appear, both their audiences and participants have become increasingly familiar with and well-versed in the forms and conventions of these shows; for example, it is now routine for participants to talk explicitly about the politics of how they are being represented at the level of the text itself. At the very least, this self-reflexivity makes it difficult to concede to the popular image of the audience for reality TV as 'unthinking voyeurs, unwitting dupes of commercialist broadcasters [and] in danger or mistaking reality-TV programmes for "reality"' (Hight, 2001: 390).

The terms and categories used to describe reality-based programming have a broader significance that extends to issues of critical, theoretical and methodological approach. In this respect, the rise of such programming can be seen to raise new challenges for, or at least ask questions of, the *existing* analytical approaches of television and cultural studies on a number of different levels (as well as their relationship with other disciplinary fields). As such, reality TV can be seen potentially to pose new questions for students and academics engaged in the study of television – how to 'pin down' texts that seem to raise such fundamental questions about the wider contexts of social, political and economic change in modern society, the political economy of television, or the medium's contemporary address to its viewers, when they may, at times, evade the grasp of conventional methodological and theoretical approaches. In addition to seeking to understand changing inflections in, and the reception of, televisual representations of 'reality' within popular factual programming, for example, another area that warrants more critical attention is the relationship *between* real crime TV and crime drama. It is intriguing to note the increasingly visible reciprocity between these modes, where a number of popular crime dramas have inspired real crime, documentary-style 'spin-offs' including *CSI: Crime Scene Investigation* (CBS, 2000–) and *The Real CSI* (5, 2004); *Prime Suspect* (Granada, 1991–2003) and *Prime Suspect: Real Life* (tx BBC1, 2001); *Cracker* (Granada, 1993–6) and *The Real Cracker* (tx C4, 2001). This kind of fluidity, which raises further significant questions about the ways audiences actually experience these programmes, is evidenced elsewhere in the way that *World's Wildest Police Videos* was made into a PlayStation video game entitled *World's Scariest Police Chases,* also featuring Sheriff John Bunnell's voice, in 2001. So too must we note the concurrent renaissance of crime drama alongside the explosion of real crime TV and examine how contemporary crime drama is also re-imagining and negotiating the boundaries of its own 'realism'; something that arguably must again be contextualised within the bigger picture of television's expanded appetite for real crime TV. It seems telling that two of the most popular drama series of recent times have done much to reconfigure realism within the crime fiction genre; where *24* (Fox, 2001–) has signalled a particular relationship with 'reality' through the conceit of real time, *CSI: Crime Scene Investigation* has done so through its close attention to forensic detail, to the privileging of *evidence* over interpretation and motive (even though the finer details of some of its scientific rigour have been questioned).

In discussing the broader cultural response to reality TV as the ultimate example of 'dumbing down' in media culture (and its consequent assumption of a 'passive' audience), Craig Hight has emphasised how such perceptions:

> typically suffer from the absence of any recognition that new theoretical tools need to be developed in order to properly understand and critique the significance of these new forms. The notion that fact-fiction hybrids such as reality-TV, docu-soaps, talk shows and reality gameshows may represent a significant and apparently permanent break from the discourses which underlie the documentary genre has been slow to arrive ... (2001: 390)

Particularly when it comes to the *study* of reality TV, this is a crucial point in developing a more sympathetic and indeed sophisticated approach to such texts. In the initial critical work on reality TV (Nichols, 1994; Dovey, 2000; Corner, 2001) there was sometimes a self-conscious debate about how to approach these texts that blur traditional generic distinctions, prompting some discussion of methodological approach. Such debate is still important; what is problematic is that even while these hybrids have become increasingly established and both academics and non-academic audiences have become versed in discussion of television's play with traditional boundaries, there is still a continuing critical and cultural discomfort around the loss of these 'distinctions'. It is now, then, that a concerted new appraisal of the 'boundaries' thought to be observed within, and adopted by, television as an organising principle warrants our attention. By moving beyond our preoccupation with 'blurring boundaries' we might more fruitfully come to understand television as a medium where these boundaries can not remain rigid and are instead consistently under construction and negotiation; and recognise that this is a process that is nowhere more evident than in real crime TV.

I started this book by 'returning to the scene of a crime' – the photo of me with a colleague in the radio studio at New Scotland Yard in 1995 – and I want to return there again as I end. In the light of all that we have seen here, this photo cannot really be called a 'fake' at all, but rather another instance of the media's ongoing appropriation, negotiation and inventiveness around the ways in which it constructs the whole spectrum of crime stories. Looking back at this picture and reflecting on the role I held then, where part of my job included locating crimes in the Metropolitan Police area that might be suitable for *Crimewatch*, I don't think I had any conception at that time of how complex, significant or influential the programme actually was then or would prove to be. As a television viewer in my early teens when the programme first appeared on British screens, by 1995 *Crimewatch* was already a programme that seemed to have been around forever for me. It was a show one could take for granted, a constant feature of the BBC's regular schedule, and even though I rarely watched it before working at New Scotland Yard, its format was unconsciously familiar and predictable to me, just as Nick Ross and Sue Cook were instantly recognisable for being its presenters.

In retrospect this alone should have indicated to me what an institution within British television the programme already was. What I did have then, however, was a slight sense of unease about it all, about its curious role in taking real crimes and having actors re-enact them for us, about its sometimes rather haughty way of addressing us, about the recurrence of and its reliance on the visibly grieving bereaved. Writing this book has done nothing to dispel any of this unease. But in seeking to understand and contextualise some of the significance of both *Crimewatch* and the subsequent rise of real crime TV, the journey from this picture has done something to underline the complex operation of generic permeability, and of televisual address and its ability to create the sense of an affirmative and inclusive community; the capacity of television to perpetuate, circulate and endorse 'common sense' ideologies; the critical, polysemic, sometimes contradictory nature of audiences' engagement with television; the necessity of continuing to revisit and reflect on the way the media represent crime and fear of crime and the myriad repercussions such representations can hold; and throughout all this, our seemingly inescapable and enduring fascination with crime stories and their resonance in our lives.

· NOTE ·

1 Furthermore, *Crimewatch*'s reconstructions are accompanied at the start by an onscreen logo that reads 'reconstruction'. However, one offender in this respect is arguably *America's Dumbest Criminals*, where much of the 'CCTV' and 'fly-on-the-wall' footage is actually re-enacted without being labelled as such; in fact, only the *authentic* material is signalled in this way, with a logo reading 'real footage'.

Works Cited

Anonymous (2001) 'Big Brother is Watching', *Metro*, 22 June, p. 41.

Auslander, Philip (1999) *Liveness: Performance in a Mediatized Culture*, London and New York: Routledge.

Baehr, Helen and Dyer, Gillian (1987) *Boxed In: Women and Television*, London: Pandora.

Barker, Dennis (1999) 'Broadcaster with Feel-Good Factor', *Guardian*, 27 April, p. 17.

Barker, Martin and Petley, Julian (1994) *Ill Effects: The Media Violence Debate*, London: Routledge.

Barthes, Roland (1993) *Camera Lucida*, London: Vintage.

BBC (n.d.) *Producers' Guidelines*, 4th edn.

BBC Broadcasting Research (1988), '*Crimewatch UK*, BBC: Special Projects Report', SP.88/45/88/16, October.

Bennett, Tony (ed.) (1981) *Popular Film and Television*, London: British Film Institute/Oxford University Press.

Benedict, Helen (1992). *Virgin or Vamp: How the Press Covers Sex Crimes*, Oxford: Oxford University Press.

Biressi, Anita (2001) *Crime, Fear and the Law in True Crime Stories*, Basingtoke: Palgrave.

—— and Nunn, Heather (2005) *Reality TV: Realism and Revelation*, London: Wallflower Press.

Bondebjerg, Ib (1996) 'Public Discourse/Private Fascination: Hybridization in "True-Life Story" Genres', *Media, Culture and Society*, vol. 18, January, pp. 27–45.

Botting, Fred (1996) *Gothic*, London and New York: Routledge.

Brenton, Sam and Cohen, Reuben (2003) *Shooting People: Adventures in Reality TV*, London and New York: Verso.

Broadcasting Standards Commission (1999–2001) Bulletins, available online at www.bsc.org.uk.

Bronfen, Elizabeth (1992) *Over her Dead Body*, Manchester: Manchester University Press.

Brooker, Will and Jermyn, Deborah (2002) *The Audience Studies Reader*, London and New York: Routledge.

Brunsdon, Charlotte (1989) 'Text and Audience', in Ellen Seiter, Hans Borchers, Gabrielle Kreutzner and Eva-Maria Warth (eds), *Remote Control: Television, Audiences and Cultural Power*, London and New York: Routledge, pp. 116–29.

——— (1997) *Screen Tastes: Soap Opera to Satellite Dishes*, London and New York: Routledge.

——— (1998) 'Structure of Anxiety: Recent British Television Crime Fiction', *Screen*, vol. 39, no. 3, pp. 223–43.

———, D'Acci, Julie and Spigel, Lynn (eds) (1997) *Feminist Television Criticism: A Reader*, Oxford: Oxford University Press.

Bruzzi, Stella (2000) *New Documentary: A Critical Introduction*, London and New York: Routledge.

Burrell, Ian (2000) '"*Crimewatch*"? It's Enough to Make you Go Out and Rob a Bank, Say Villains', *Independent*, 1 July, p. 9.

Byerly, Caroline M. (1999) 'News, Feminism and the Dialectics of Gender Relations', in, Marian Meyers (ed.), *Mediated Women: Representations in Popular Culture*, Cresskill, NJ: Hampton Press, pp. 382–403.

Campbell, Duncan (1993a) 'Big Brother is Here', *Guardian* (G2), 13 May, p. 2.

——— (1993b) 'Murder Suspect Goes Free at 11th Hour', *Guardian*, 12 November, p. 26.

——— (1994a) 'Who Stabbed Michael Winner in the Back?', *Guardian*, 31 August, p. 16.

——— (1994b) 'Sky Tries to Make Crime Pay', *Guardian*, 19 September, p. 13.

Carter, Cynthia (1998a) 'News of Sexual Violence against Women and Girls in the British Daily National Press', PhD thesis, Cardiff University.

——— (1998b) 'When the "Extraordinary" Becomes "Ordinary": Everyday News of Sexual Violence', in Cynthia Carter, Gill Branston and Stuart Allan (eds), *News, Gender and Power*, London and New York: Routledge, pp. 219–32.

———, Branston, Gill and Allan, Stuart (eds) (1998) *News, Gender and Power*, London and New York: Routledge.

Carter, Meg (1998) 'Time for a Reality Check', *Broadcast*, 18 September, pp. 16–17.

Cashmore, Ellis (1994) *... And There Was Television*, London: Routledge.

Cathcart, Brian (2001) *Jill Dando: Her Life and Murder*, London: Penguin.

Caughie, John (1981) 'Progressive Television and Documentary Drama', in Tony Bennett (ed.), *Popular Film and Television*, London: British Film Institute/Oxford University Press, 327–52.

Cavender, Gray (2004) 'In Search of Community on Reality TV: *America's Most Wanted* and *Survivor*', in Su Holmes and Deborah Jermyn (eds), *Understanding Reality Television*, London and New York: Routledge, pp. 154–72.

—— and Bond-Maupin, Lisa (1993) 'Fear and Loathing on Reality Television: An Analysis of "*America's Most Wanted*" and "*Unsolved Mysteries*"', *Sociological Inquiry*, vol. 63 no. 3, pp. 305–17.

——, —— and Jurik, Nancy C. (1999) 'The Construction of Gender in Reality Crime TV', *Gender and Society*, vol. 13, no. 5, October, pp. 643–63.

Chesney-Lind, Meda (1997) *The Female Offender: Girls, Women and Crime*, Thousand Oaks, CA: Sage.

Chibnall, Steve (1977) *Law and Order News: An Analysis of Crime Reporting in the British Press*, London: Tavistock.

Clark, Bernard (2002) 'The Box of Tricks', in Dolan Cummings (ed.), *Reality TV: How Real is Real?*, Oxford: Hodder and Stoughton, pp. 1–16.

Clarke, Alan (1992) '"You're Nicked!" Television Police Series and the Fictional Representation of Law and Order', in Dominic Strinati and Stephen Wagg (eds), *Come On Down? Popular Media Culture in Post-War Britain*, London: Routledge, pp. 233–53.

Clissold, Bradley D. (2004) '*Candid Camera* and the Origins of Reality TV: Contextualising a Historical Precedent', in Su Holmes and Deborah Jermyn (eds), *Understanding Reality Television*, London and New York: Routledge, pp. 33–53.

Connet, David (1994) 'Winner's Crime Show Loses Out to its Critics', *Daily Mail*, 30 August, p. 7.

Corner, John (1999) *Critical Ideas in Television Studies*, Oxford: Oxford University Press.

—— (2001) 'Documentary in a Post-Documentary Culture? A Note on Forms and Their Functions' available at http://www.lboro.ac.uk/research/changing.media/John%20Corner%20paper.htm, (accesssed 3 January 2003).

Couldry, Nick (2003) *Media Rituals: A Critical Approach*, London and New York: Routledge.

Cubitt, Sean (1991) *Timeshift: On Video Culture*, London and New York: Routledge.

Culf, Andrew (1993) 'BBC Defends "Voyeuristic" Crime Series', *Guardian*, 23 June, p. 6.

—— (1994) 'BBC Tones Down Crime Coverage', *Guardian*, 2 June, p. 4.

Dauncey, Hugh (1996) 'French Reality Television: More than a Matter of Taste?', *European Journal of Communication*, vol. 11, no. 1, pp. 83–106.

—— (1998) '"Témoin No. 1": Crime Shows on French Television', in Mark Fishman, and Gray Cavender (eds), *Entertaining Crime: Television Reality Programs*, New York: Aldine De Gruyter, pp. 193–209.

Dayan, Daniel and Katz, Elihu (1994) *Media Events: The Live Broadcasting of History*, Cambridge, MA, and London: Harvard University Press.

Davenport, Justin (1999) 'One Shot from a Silenced Gun', *Evening Standard*, 27 April, p. 2.

Derosia, Margaret (2002) 'The Court of Last Resort: Making Race, Crime and Nation on *America's Most Wanted*', in James Friedman (ed.), *Reality Squared: Televisual Discourse on the Real*, New Brunswick, NJ: Rutgers University Press, pp. 236–55.

Dienst, Richard (1994) *Still Life in Real Time*, Durham, NC, and London: Duke University Press.

Dovey, John (2000) *Freakshow: First Person Media and Factual TV*, London: Pluto Press.

Du Maurier, Daphne (1938) *Rebecca*, London: Pan.

Edgar, David (1982) 'On Drama Documentary', in F. Pike (ed.), *Ah! Mischief: The Writer and Television*, London: Faber and Faber, pp. 14–29.

Edwards, Jeff (1999) 'Who Was the Hitman?' *Mirror*, 27 April, p. 4.

Ellis, John (1994) *Visible Fictions*, London and New York: Routledge, 2nd edn.

—— (2000) *Seeing Things: Television in the Age of Uncertainty*, London and New York: I.B.Tauris.

Fairclough, Norman (1995) *Media Discourse*, London: Arnold.

Faludi, Susan (1991) *Backlash: The Undeclared War Against Women*. London: Chatto and Windus.

Fetveit, Arild (1999) 'Reality TV in the Digital Era: A Paradox in Visual Culture?', *Media, Culture and Society*, vol. 21, no. 6, pp. 787–804.

Feuer, Jane (1983) 'The Concept of Live Television: Ontology as Ideology', in E. Ann Kaplan (ed.), *Regarding Television*, Los Angeles: American Film Institute, pp. 12–22.

Fiddick, Peter (1992) 'Research', *Guardian*, 6 April, p. 31.

Fishman, Mark (1998) 'Ratings and Reality: The Persistence of the Reality Crime Genre', in Mark Fishman and Gray Cavender (eds), *Entertaining Crime: Television Reality Programmes*, New York: Aldine de Gruyter, pp. 59–75.

—— and Cavender, Gray (eds) (1998) *Entertaining Crime: Television Reality Programmes*, New York: Aldine de Gruyter.

Fiske, John (1987) *Television Culture*, London: Methuen.

Foucault, Michel (1991) *Discipline and Punish: The Birth of the Prison*, London: Penguin.

Friedman, James (ed.) (2002) *Reality Squared: Televisual Discourse on the Real*, New Brunswick, NJ: Rutgers University Press.

Fyfe, Nicholas R. and Bannister, Jon (1998) 'The Eyes Upon the Street – Closed-Circuit Television Surveillance and the City', in Nicholas R. Fyfe and Jon Bannister (eds), *Images of the Street: Planning, Identity and Control in Public Space*, London and New York: Routledge, pp. 254–67.

Garland, D. (1991) *Punishment and Modern Society: A Study in Social Theory*, Oxford: Clarendon Press.

Gatrell, J. A. C. (1994*) The Hanging Tree: Execution and the English People 1770–1868*, Oxford: Oxford University Press.

Garnham, Nick (1971) 'TV Documentary and Ideology', *Screen Reader One*, SEFT, pp. 55–61.

Geraghty, Christine (1991) *Women and Soap Opera: A Study of Prime Time Soaps*, Cambridge: Polity.

Gerbner, George and Gross, Larry (1976) 'Living with Television – The Violence Profile', *Journal of Communication*, vol. 26, no. 2, Spring, pp. 173–99.

Gilbert, Sandra M. and Gubar, Susan (1984) *The Madwoman in the Attic: The Woman Writer and the Nineteenth Century Literary Imagination*, New Haven, CT, and London: Yale University Press.

Gray, Ann (1987), 'Behind Closed Doors: Video Recorders in the Home', in Helen Baehr and Gillian Dyer (eds), *Boxed In: Women and Television*, New York and London: Pandora, pp. 38–54.

Graham, Polly (1994) 'Double Barrel; The Column that Gives Vitriol a Bad Name', *Guardian*, 19 August, p. 13.

Green, Nick (1994) 'Happy Birthday: You're Nicked', *Daily Mail*, 7 August, p. 31.

Gunning, Tom (1990) 'The Cinema of Attractions: Early Film, Its Spectators and the Avant-Garde', in Thomas Elsaesser and Adam Barker (eds), *Early Cinema: Space, Frame, Narrative*, London: British Film Institute, pp. 56–62.

——— (1995) 'Tracing the Individual Body: Photography, Detectives and Early Cinema', in Leo Charney and Vannessa Schwartz (eds), *Cinema and the Invention of Modern Life*, Berkeley and Los Angeles: University of California Press, pp. 15–45.

Gunter, Barrie (1987) *Television and the Fear of Crime*, London: John Libbey and Company Ltd.

Hall, Stuart (1972) 'The Determinants of News Photographs', *Working Papers in Cultural Studies*, no. 3, pp. 53–87.

——— (1978) *Policing the Crisis: Mugging, the State and Law and Order*, London: Macmillan Education.

——— (1983) 'The Great Moving Right Show', in Stuart Hall and Martin Jacques (eds), *The Politics of Thatcherism*, London: Lawrence and Wishart, pp. 19–39.

——— and Jacques, Martin (eds) (1983) *The Politics of Thatcherism*, London: Lawrence and Wishart.

Hamilton, Peter and Hargreaves, Roger (2001) *The Beautiful and the Damned: The Creation of Identity in Nineteenth Century Photography*, Aldershot: Lund Humphries.

Harrison, Tracey (1994) 'Nick Ross Eats his Words in Clash with Winner', *Daily Mail*, 29 August, p. 3.

Hartley, John (1982) *Understanding News*, London and New York: Routledge.

—— (1992) *The Politics of Pictures*, London : Routledge.

—— (1998) 'Juvenation: News, Girls and Power', in Cynthia Carter, Gill Branston and Stuart Allan (eds), *News, Gender and Power*, London and New York: Routledge, pp. 47–70.

Hebert, Hugh (1993) 'The People's Peepshow', *Guardian*, 23 November, p. 6.

Henning, Michelle (1997) 'The Subject as Object: Photography and the Human Body', in Liz Wells (ed.), *Photography: A Critical Introduction*, London: Routledge, pp. 217–48.

Hepburn, Ian and Crosbie, Paul (1999) 'Was it Revenge of *Crimewatch* Crook?', *Sun*, 27 April, pp. 12–13.

Hight, Craig (2001) 'Debating Reality-TV', *Continuum: Journal of Media and Cultural Studies*, vol. 15, no. 3, pp. 389–95.

Hill, Amelia (2001) '*Crimewatch* Presenter Attacks Police Methods', *Observer*, 21 October, p. 7.

Hill, Annette (1996) *Shocking Entertainment*, Luton: University of Luton Press.

—— (2000) 'Crime and Crisis: British Reality TV in Action', in Ed Buscombe (ed.), *British Television: A Reader*, Oxford: Oxford University Press, pp. 218–34.

—— (2005) *Reality TV: Audiences and Popular Factual Television*, London: Routledge.

—— and Palmer, Gareth (2002) 'Editorial: Big Brother', *Television and New Media*, vol. 3, no. 3, pp. 323–31.

Hirsch, P. (1980) 'The Scary World of the Non-Viewer and Other Anomalies: A Re-Analysis of Gerbner et al's Findings on Cultivation Analysis: Part I', *Communication Research*, vol. 7, pp. 403–56.

The History of Surveillance (2001) (video recording) tx C4, 8 April.

Holland, Patricia (1991) 'History, Memory and the Family Album', in Patricia Holland and Jo Spence (eds), *Family Snaps: The Meanings of Domestic Photography*, London: Virago, pp. 1–14.

Holmes, Su and Jermyn, Deborah (2004) (eds) *Understanding Reality Television*, London and New York: Routledge.

Hughes, M. (1980) 'The Fruits of Cultivation Analysis: A Re-Examination of the Effects of Television in Fear of Victimisation, Alienation and Approval of Violence', *Public Opinion Quarterly*, vol. 44, pp. 287–302.

Ingrams, Richard (1994) 'War Can Never Be Right-On', *Observer*, 27 March, p. 28.

Izod, John, Kilborn, Richard and Hibberd, Matthew (2000) *From Grierson to the Docu-Soap: Breaking the Boundaries*, Luton: University of Luton Press.

James, Nick (2003) 'Horror Movie', *Sight and Sound*, vol. 3, no. 2, February, pp. 20–2.

Jermyn, Deborah (1995) 'An Appealing Solution', *Metropolitan Journal*, no. 12, January, pp. 32–3.

—— (2001) 'Death of the Girl Next Door: Celebrity, Femininity and Tragedy in the Murder of Jill Dando', *Feminist Media Studies*, vol. 1, no. 3, November, pp. 343–59.

—— (2003) 'Women with a Mission: Lynda La Plante, DCI Jane Tennison and the Reinvention of Television Crime Drama', *International Journal of Cultural Studies*, vol. 6, no. 1, March, pp. 46–63.

—— (2006) 'Fact, Fiction and Everything in Between: Negotiating Boundaries in *Crimewatch UK*', in Jacqueline Furby and Karen Randell (eds), *Screen Method: Comparative Readings in Screen Studies*, London: Wallflower Press, pp. 145–56.

Kettle, Martin (1983) 'The Drift to Law and Order' in Stuart Hall and Martin Jacques (eds), *The Politics of Thatcherism*, London: Lawrence and Wishart.

Kerr, Paul (1990) 'F for Fake? Friction over Faction', in Gary Whannel (ed.), *Understanding Television*, London: Routledge, pp. 75–87.

Kidd Hewitt, David and Osborne, Richard (eds) (1995) *Crime and the Media: The Post Modern Spectacle*, London: Pluto.

Kilborn, Richard (1994) 'How Real Can You Get?: Recent Developments in "Reality' Television"', *European Journal of Communication*, vol. 9, pp. 421–39.

—— (2003) *Staging the Real: Factual TV Programming in the Age of Big Brother*, Manchester: Manchester University Press.

Kilgour, Maggie (1995) *The Rise of the Gothic Novel*, London and New York: Routledge.

Kuhn, Annette (1995) *Family Secrets: Acts of Memory and Imagination*, London: Verso.

Leishman, Frank and Mason, Paul (2003) *Policing and the Media: Facts, Fictions and Factions*, Devon: Willan Publishing.

Lloyd, Ann (1995) *Doubly Deviant, Doubly Damned*, Harmondsworth: Penguin.

Lury, Karen (2005) *Interpreting Television*, London: Hodder Education.

Lydall, Ross (2003) 'Cameras Will Push Crime into Suburbs', *Evening Standard*, 3 February, p. 18.

Marshall, P. David (1997) *Celebrity and Power*, Minneapolis: University of Minnesota Press.

Mason, Paul (ed.) (2003) *Criminal Visions: Media Representations of Crime and Justice*, Devon: Willan Publishing.

McLean, Gareth (2002) 'No Flagging in Urge to Peep through the Keyhole', *Guardian*, 7 September, p. 7.

Mathiesen, T. (1997) 'The Viewer Society: Michel Foucault's "Panopticon" Revisited', *Theoretical Criminology*, vol. 1, no. 2, pp. 215–34.

Mawby, Rob C. (2001) 'Promoting the Police? The Rise of Police Image Work', *Criminal Justice Matters*, no. 43, Spring, pp. 44–5.

Metropolitan Police (2001) (Information Pack) *'Enough is Enough': Domestic Violence Strategy*, London: Metropolitan Police.

Meyers, Marian (1997) *News Coverage of Violence Against Women: Engendering Blame*, London: Sage.

—— (ed.) (1999) *Mediated Women: Representations in Popular Culture*, Cresskill, NJ: Hampton Press.

Miller, Hugh (2001) *Crimewatch Solved: The Inside Story*, Basingstoke: Boxtree.

Miller, Tim (2001) Series producer of *Britain's Most Wanted*, interviewed (with Jo Scarratt) at LWT offices, London, 2 April.

Miller, Susan L. (1998) *Crime Control and Women: Feminist Implications of Criminal Justice Policy*, London: Sage.

Mills, Liz (1993) 'Accuracy and Reconstructions', *Guardian*, 2 December, p. 25.

Minogue, Kenneth and Biddiss, Michael (eds) (1987) *Thatcherism: Personality and Politics*, Basingstoke: Macmillan Press.

Minogue, Tim (1990) 'Putting Real Crime on Prime Time', *Guardian*, 3 September, p. 23.

Modleski, Tania (1988) *Loving with a Vengeance: Mass Produced Fantasies for Women*, New York, London: Routledge.

Moers, Ellen (1986) *Literary Women*, London: Women's Press.

Moore, Jane (1999) 'She Was Decent, Warm, Even Ordinary, But That was her Charm', *Sun*, 27 April, p. 7.

—— and Parker, Andrew (1999) 'Anguish of Pal Anthea', *Sun*, 27 April, p. 10.

Morrison, Anne (1992) (letters to editor), *Guardian*, 14 July, p. 20.

Morrison, David E., Mcgregor, Brent, Svennevig, Michael and Firmstone, Julie (1999) *Defining Violence; The Search for Understanding*, Luton: University of Luton Press.

Myers, Alice and Wight, Sarah (eds) (1996) *No Angels: Women Who Commit Violence*, London: Pandora.

Naffine, Ngaire (1997) *Feminism and Criminology*, Cambridge: Polity.

Nichols, Bill (1994) *Blurred Boundaries; Questions of Meaning in Contemporary Culture*, Bloomington: Indiana University Press.

O'Neill, Sean (1999) 'Blind Date Produced a Joy to Match Career Success', *Daily Telegraph*, 27 April, p. 3.

O'Sullivan, Kevin (1999) 'Gawky Kid who Became a Screen Beauty', *Mirror*, 27 April, p. 10.

Palmer, Gareth (2003) *Discipline and Liberty: Television and Governance*, Manchester: Manchester University Press.

Paterson, Peter (1994) 'Flaw in the Nick of Time', *Daily Mail*, 6 July, p. 11.

Perkins Gilman, Charlotte (1892) *The Yellow Wallpaper*, in Ann J. Lane (ed.), *The Charlotte Perkins Gilman Reader*, London: Women's Press, pp. 3–26.

Pharo, Chris (1999) 'Family She Adored', *Sun*, 27 April, p. 9.

Phillips, Belinda (2002) Assistant producer of *Crimewatch UK*, interviewed at BBC offices, London, 19 February.

Radway, Janice (1984) *Reading the Romance: Women, Patriarchy and Popular Literature*, Chapel Hill, NC, and London: University of North Carolina Press.

Rath, Claus-Deiter (1985) 'The Invisible Network: Television as an Institution in Everyday Life', in P. Drummond and R. Paterson (eds), *Television in Transition,* London: British Film Institute, pp. 199–204.

—— (1988) 'Live/Life: Television as a Generator of Events in Everyday Life', in Philip Drummond (ed.), *Television and its Audiences: International Research Perspectives*, London: British Film Institute, pp. 32–7.

—— (1989) 'Live Television and its Audiences: Challenges of Media Reality', in Ellen Seiter, Hans Borchers, Gabrielle Kreutzner and Eva-Maria Warth (eds), *Remote Control: Television, Audiences and Cultural Power*, London and New York: Routledge, pp. 79–95.

Raymond, Clare (1999) 'TV Nick Sobs for Friend', *Mirror*, 27 April, p. 5.

Robins, Kevin (1995) 'Will Image Move Us Still?', in Martin Lister (ed.), *The Photographic Image in Digital Culture*, London and New York: Routledge, pp. 29–50.

Roscoe, Jane (2001) 'Big Brother Australia: Performing the "Real" Twenty-four-Seven', *International Journal of Cultural Studies*, vol. 4, no. 4, pp. 473–88.

—— and Hight, Craig (2001) *Faking It: Mock Documentary and the Subversion of Factuality*, Manchester: Manchester University Press.

Ross, Jean (1992) 'First Person: Home Alone', *Guardian*, 26 February, p. 13.

Ross, Nick (1999) 'Talented, Beautiful and Brimming with Integrity', *Daily Telegraph*, 27 April, p. 3.

—— and Cook, Sue (1987) *Crimewatch UK*, London: Hodder and Stoughton.

Seabrook, Jeremy (1991) 'My Life is in that Box', in Patricia Holland and Jo Spence (eds), *Family Snaps: The Meanings of Domestic Photography*, London: Virago, pp. 171–85.

Scarratt, Jo (2001) Producer of *Britain's Most Wanted*, interviewed at LWT offices, London, 2 April.

Schlesinger, Philip (1995) *Reporting Crime*, Oxford: Clarendon Press.

——, Dobash, R. Emerson, Dobash, Russell P. and Weaver, C. Kay (1992) *Women Viewing Violence*, London: British Film Institute.

——— and Tumber, Howard (1993) 'Fighting the War Against Crime; Television, Police and Audience, *British Journal of Criminology*, vol. 33, no. 1, pp. 19–32.

Schwartz, Vanessa (1995) 'Cinematic Spectatorship Before the Apparatus: The Public Taste for Reality in Fin-de-Siècle Paris', in Leo Charney and Vannessa Schwartz (eds), *Cinema and the Invention of Modern Life*, Berkeley and Los Angeles: University of California Press, pp. 297–319.

Showalter, Elaine (2000) *The Female Malady*, London: Virago.

Smart, Carol (1980) *Women, Crime and Criminology: A Feminist Critique*, London: Routledge.

Smith, Christine and Rae, Charles (1999) 'She Was the Best Sobs Nick', *Sun*, 27 April, p. 4.

Sontag, Susan (1979) *On Photography*, London: Penguin.

Soothill, Keith (1995) 'Sex Crime News from Abroad', in R. Emmerson Dobash, Russell P. Dobash and Lesley Noaks (eds), *Gender and Crime*, Cardiff: University of Wales Press, pp. 96–114.

——— and Walby, Sylvia (1991) *Sex Crime in the News*, London and New York: Routledge.

Sparks, Richard (1992) *Television and the Drama of Crime: Moral Tales and the Place of Crime in Public Life*, Buckingham and Philadelphia: Open University Press.

Stanko, Elizabeth (1990) *Everyday Violence*, London: Pandora.

——— (1992) 'The Case of Fearful Women: Gender, Personal Safety and Fear of Crime', *Women and Criminal Justice*, vol. 4, no. 1, pp 117–35.

Sullivan, Mike and Hughes, Simon (1999) 'Assasinated', *Sun*, 27 April, pp. 1–3.

Tagg, John (1988) *The Burden of Representation: Essays on Photographies and Histories*, Basingstoke and London: Macmillan.

Tomc, Sandra (1995) 'Questing Women: The Feminist Mystery after Feminism', in Glenwood Irons (ed.), *Feminism in Women's Detective Fiction*, Toronto: University of Toronto Press, pp. 47–63.

Thomson, Katie (2002) Series producer of *Crimewatch UK*, personal interview at BBC offices, London, 22 January.

Tincknell, Estella and Raghuram, Parvati (2002) *'Big Brother*: Reconfiguring the "Active" Audience of Cultural Studies?', *European Journal of Cultural Studies*, vol. 5, no. 2, pp. 199–215.

Toon, Ian (2000) '"Finding a Place in the Street": CCTV Surveillance and Young People's Use of Urban Public Space', in David Bell and Azzedine Haddour (eds), *City Visions*, Essex: Prentice Hall, Pearson Education, pp. 141–65.

Toynbee, Polly (1994) 'The Channels of Fear', *Guardian*, 3 June, p. 20.

Trachtenburg, Alan (1980) *Classic Essays on Photography*, New Haven, CT: Leete's Island Books.

Tulloch, John (2000) '"Landscapes of Fear": Public Places, Fear of Crime and the Media', in Stuart Allan, Gill Branston and Cynthia Carter (eds), *Environmental Risks and the Media*, London: Routledge, pp. 184–97.

Urrichio, William and Pearson, Roberta E. (1993) *Reframing Culture*, Princeton, NJ: Princeton University Press.

van Zoonen, Liesbet (1998) 'One of the Girls?; The Changing Gender of Journalism', in Cynthia Carter, Gill Branston and Stuart Allan (eds), *News, Gender and Power*, London and New York: Routledge, pp. 33–46.

Walklate, Sandra (1995) *Gender and Crime: An Introduction*, Hemel Hempstead: Prentice Hall.

Weaver, C. Kay (1998) *'Crimewatch UK*: Keeping Women Off the Streets', in Cynthia Carter, Gill Branston and Stuart Allan (eds), *News, Gender and Power*, London and New York: Routledge, pp. 248–62.

——, Carter, Cynthia and Stanko, Elizabeth (2000). 'The Female Body at Risk: Media, Sexual Violence and the Gendering of Public Environments', in Stuart Allan, Barbara Adam and Cynthia Carter (eds), *Environmental Risks and the Media*, London and New York: Routledge, pp. 171–83.

Wheatley, Helen (2001) 'Real Crime Television in the 8–9 Slot – Consuming Fear', in Charlotte Brunsdon, Catherine Johnson, Rachel Moseley and Helen Wheatley, 'Factual Entertainment on British Television', *European Journal of Cultural Studies*, vol. 4, no. 1, February, pp. 29–62.

Williams, Raymond (1975) *Television: Technology and Cultural Form*, New York: Schoken Books.

Winston, Brian (1996) *Technologies of Seeing: Photography, Cinematography and Television*, London: British Film Institute.

Wober, J. M. and Gunter, B. (1990) 'Crime Reconstruction Programmes: Viewing Experience in Three Regions, Linked with Perceptions of and Reactions to Crime', IBA Research Paper, GPC/03977, August.

Woffinden, Bob (1989) 'Crime Time Viewing', *The Listener*, vol. 112, no. 3139, 9 November, pp. 9–10.

Woolley, Benjamin (1984) 'An Arresting Programme', *The Listener*, vol. 112, no. 2072, 23 August. p. 11.

Index